CECIL B. MURPHEY

put on a happy faith!

Christian Herald Books
40 Overlook Drive, Chappaqua, New York 10514

To Shirley and the Scribe Tribe

Foreword

Take your choice: the Church of the Long Face or the Order of the Perpetual Grin. Most Christians belong to one or the other.

The Long-Face Congregation points to sadness in the world. Heartache is everywhere. Their lives reflect misery and discouragement. Beauty scarcely touches their drab existence. Jesus will make them happy one day, but not today.

Members of the Perpetual Grin are different. Smiles lay frozen on their faces. Never any real problems. "Everything's all right" is their resounding reply. Heartaches daunt them not. "Victory in Jesus" is the only phrase of importance in their vocabulary. They dare not tell you how many tears flow or how deep the ache.

Life is not always grins and giggles. Neither is it all sorrow and sadness. Possibilities for authentic happiness or honest despair constantly confront us.

Jesus said, "Be of good cheer, I have overcome the world!" Translated today, his words might read, "Be happy!" He promises abundant life for his people, now and forever.

The Greek word *markarios,* normally translated "blessed" has several meanings. When used in this book I have translated it "happy." This is not only a possible translation but, in my opinion, a far more meaningful one. I have offered my own translations in many places in this book to give a new perspective to some familiar verses; otherwise I quote from the Revised Standard Version.

You can be a happy Christian! There is a way to happiness. It is through Jesus Christ who offers the antidotes to spiritual depression and failure.

put on a happy faith!

put on
a happy
faith!

1

*Happy are the poor in spirit, for
theirs is the kingdom of heaven.*

MATTHEW 5:3

BY BEING POOR

"That's it," beamed Martha. "We'll celebrate. You got a five dollar raise and we ought to do something special."

"Like what?" mumbled her spouse.

"Let's buy a new sofa set. This gray monster makes the room drab. With new living room furniture I would be completely happy."

George and Martha bought the suite.

A month later she said, "Dear, I'm so pleased with the set. But, have you noticed our threadbare carpet? We ought to buy a new one." And they did.

They added lamps and drapes—after all, why cheapen the effect of new furniture?

"George, I'm happy with our beautiful living room. But . . . I could be perfectly content if we had a new dining room table and chairs. This one is too old-fashioned. It's full of scratches, and it was cheap to begin with."

But Household Finance, FHA, Bank Americard and Master Charge did not rejoice in this newly-acquired happiness. Bills rolled in, and the couple was worse off than before. Their mistake was common. George and Martha looked for happiness in objects. "If only we had" cursed their lives. The more they possessed, the more possessed they became. Sadly many of us, too, learn that

3

happiness is not found in what we own. "Happy are the poor in Spirit," said Jesus.

"Aha!" Harry cries. "Now I see! I'll give away everything I own. Then by living frugally . . ."

No, that's not the way either. Jesus said, "Happy are the poor *in spirit.*" The Lord speaks not of income or output, getting or giving, having or not having. He is talking about the condition of the heart.

Characteristic of these truly happy people is an absence of pride. The poor in heart are those who recognize a sense of need in themselves. They perceive their lack of spiritual maturity. They recognize themselves as being less than what God calls them to become. Unable to boast of great achievements, they try to be like Jesus, the Great Example. Jesus did miracles and healed the sick, but at the same time declared, "I can do nothing on my own authority" (John 5:30). The poor in spirit recognize the good they do accomplish comes from God.

Betty works tirelessly for others. When anyone is sick, Betty comes. Money problems? A shoulder to cry on? Betty makes herself available. She quietly goes through life, telling no one of her helping hands. Other church members scarcely know she gets involved in the lives of so many. God works through Betty, bringing untold solace to troubled souls.

She doesn't acknowledge or accept this. Once I asked, "Betty, what is your contribution to the kingdom of God?"

"Nothing much," she replied. It was not a kind of false humility.

She did not recognize value in her efforts. Betty does not believe she does anything of lasting significance for God's kingdom. This is *not* poverty of spirit. The spiritually poor see themselves realistically. They know their worth to God. They also know their need of Him.

4

Erasto exemplified such an attitude. He taught us a difficult African dialect, guided us in matters of etiquette, and loved us as a brother in Christ. This African teacher saw himself quite honestly. One day he shared with us a testimony of a church he had pioneered.

"Our church is progressing nicely and the people are putting forth their best. I have done a good job and the people like me. The Holy Spirit has worked in many hearts."

Erasto neither boasted nor denied with a false humility. He worked hard and acknowledged it. Yet this young man also realized that God had worked in all his efforts. Erasto knew his own weaknesses (which were also shared with us), but he knew his worth. That's poverty of spirit.

Paul wrote, "I worked harder than any of them," (I Corinthians 15:10). Boastful? Not at all. He wrote as he saw himself. "Though it was not I, but the grace of God which is with me" (v. 10b). Why put on a false humility?

Jacob was a shyster of the worst sort. If a trickier way could be found, undoubtedly he would learn it. One night Jacob reached the place of uncertainty. Gone was all self-assurance. Jacob knew his brother Esau, whom he had defrauded, would arrive in the morning. Esau had sworn vengeance. Jacob feared the impending confrontation. A return to the area of Haran was impossible: his in-laws would offer no welcome. Jacob feared to go forward because of his brother's certain wrath.

That night a heaven-sent messenger appeared to Jacob (see Genesis 32:22–31). Exactly what occured we cannot be certain. But the lesson we know. The Jacob who wrestled with the "man" was subdued. He left the river Jabbok a new person. From then on he was "Israel" (a prince with God) and forgotten was "Jacob" (deceiver). No longer was he self-reliant and filled with ideas of cheating. He hobbled away, a beaten man, yet he was one who henceforth served God. This is poverty of spirit.

Peter of the Gospels is depicted as a braggadocio. He is fully assured of his courage to face temptations. He boasts, "Lord, I'll not let you down. Even if others deny you, I'll remain faithful." Famous last words! Peter denied Jesus time and again when actually put to the test.

In the Book of Acts the Spirit-filled Peter emerges as a new man. No longer self-assertive, he now relies on God's power. While never ceasing to be bold, he becomes aware of the source of his strength. "Why do you stare at us, as though by our own power or piety we had made him walk?" (Acts 3:12), asks Peter. He disclaims the ability to heal a lame man. God, Peter contends, heals; not man.

In Philippians chapter three, Paul writes of himself, listing many reasons for pride. He is highly educated, from a significant family, devoutly religious. After recounting his "advantages," he concludes: "All this is garbage" (see Philippians 3:8). These things hold no significance for him. In fact, they hinder his relationship to Jesus Christ. Paul says in another place, "By the grace of God I am what I am" (I Corinthians 15:10). In Romans 15:17–18 he writes, "In Christ Jesus, then, I have reason to be proud of my work for God. For I will not venture to speak of anything except what Christ has wrought through me." Acknowledging his own insufficiency, Paul evidences genuine poverty of spirit.

When Jesus calls the poor in spirit happy, he makes a *pronouncement,* not a promise. The poor in spirit are blessed *now.* Because of their sense of spiritual impoverishment, they accept themselves for what they are. Christ blesses that honesty.

By nature I am a compulsive and hardworking person. "You can't be satisfied with getting a job done tomorrow —you want it done yesterday," my wife Shirley remarked once.

People with my characteristics get results—but often they see them as the outcome of their own efforts. God is involved somewhere, but results are the natural corollary of diligence. Concepts of failure seldom threaten people like me—we can do any task to which we set ourselves. It's humbling to admit that success occurs by God's goodness.

A few years ago one of those bad weeks hit. Every night was filled with either a scheduled meeting or frantic calls for help. I was out till the late hours each night. The phone awakened Shirley and me early. Rush. Push. Drive. By Saturday night my sermon still had not been prepared. Shame and guilt disturbed me.

By Sunday morning my body rebelled with exhaustion. Church attendance was smaller than usual. Drizzles of rain screened the sun's appearance. An emergency had called the organist out of town. His substitute played hymns of praise as though intended for a funeral dirge. It was a rotten day.

I preached that morning: a poor message delivered with a great deal of inner trembling. "You sure missed it today," I muttered to myself after the final "Amen."

As I stood by the door to shake hands with the faithful few, almost everyone had some response. "That was a helpful message," ventured one. "Oh, I felt you were talking just to me," commented a young lady. "I can't remember when I've enjoyed a sermon so much," chimed in a deacon.

Walking from the church my steps were a little lighter. God had taken an ill-prepared sermon and used it to bless people. It was a humbling lesson. My efforts counted—but in the long run it was God who made the message meaningful.

In honesty I have to tell the next installment of the story. The following Sunday could have been a repeat performance. The difference was that the tension had eased, giving me time for study, but I purposely walked into the pulpit with insufficient preparation.

At the door, one or two people smiled. Most of them merely shook hands. Two commented on the fine weather!

Poverty of spirit! This is one of the secrets of happiness. We work as God gives abilities and talents. The results are his. Christ leaves no grounds for either self-boasting or self-denial. Christians are called for service. Our efforts *alone* prove fruitless. "Without me you can do nothing," our Lord reminds us (John 15:5). The work of the Christian is not for his own pleasure nor for the exclusive pleasure of others. His service is for God to use as a means of blessing the world in which he lives.

By accepting our effectiveness and our limitations, we grasp that Jesus is the All-Sufficient One. Isn't that real happiness?

2

*Happy are those who mourn, for
they shall be comforted.*

MATTHEW 5:4

BY MOURNING

A sudden thunderstorm rages in the middle of the night.
Lights glare from an on-coming car. A half-dazed driver
rapidly spins the wheel. Too late! James, asleep in the
back seat, is the only survivor of both vehicles.

Later friends crowd about the young man, offering
comfort and consolation. "Keep a stiff upper lip."
"Don't let this get you down." "Just don't think about
it."

James trys to heed their advice, drying tears that want
to flow. He forces his mind to other matters when he
wants to mourn.

"You're really holding up fine, Jim!" says one ac-
quaintance.

"Sure admire your courage—the way you've taken all
this!" says another.

One wiser friend visits James. Phil notices the quiver-
ing lips and a voice tending toward huskiness. James'
eyes mist as he talks.

"It hurts, doesn't it?" Phil says to his bereaved friend.

That's all he spoke. Yet those few words established a
bond of understanding between them. Phil felt James'
grief.

Afterwards James remarked, "I feel a burden has been
lifted."

Mourning brings its own comfort and aids in healing. Facing up to grief is the beginning of a therapeutic process. Accepting loss starts the process leading to peace. Tears, anger, shouts—any genuine emotion genuinely expressed—is a way of working out inner feelings. In giving vent to emotions we can find relief and release.

Life for each of us looms as a mixture of heartache and joy. Part of living as mature adults means accepting life as it is: bliss and pain, harmony coupled with disunity. No life exists without difficulties, but facing life's contradictions brings happiness. In admitting discouragement we discover comfort.

The experience of sorrow constitutes a necessary part of the process of making a person. Sorrow has its own blessedness to give. Through feeling pain ourselves, we can understand another who is ill. Can the totally rich experience the hunger of the poor? Only those who have grieved can empathize with those who mourn the loss of a loved one.

This is all true. Yet I believe Jesus spoke of something far deeper. His gift of happiness is for those who mourn for themselves. They sense their failures and want to do something about them. They grieve because they have not fully lived up to their understanding of God's claims on their lives.

On the mission field we were hundreds of miles from a city where good reading material could be purchased. As Shirley and I met other missionaries we usually got acquainted with them largely through the books in their libraries. A British couple had the largest library in that province. We became close friends and saw each other regularly. Visits concluded with an armload of books to read. On one occasion I borrowed a book written in the last century. It was *Holiness,* by John Ryle, an Anglican bishop.

After reading only the introduction and first chapter I laid it aside, unable to go on.

Something happened in the reading of those dozen pages. Conviction of sin and failure overwhelmed me.

Why? That was a hard question to answer. As a missionary my efforts met with success. Relationships with the Africans were warm. No other missionary worked any harder for the sake of the Gospel. As a matter of fact, I probably worked harder than most. It was a good feeling to be a successful and respected missionary.

Unable to return to the book, I sat there, surveying the situation. I had seen outstanding results: evidence of conversions and dedications. People had actually been healed in their bodies and minds. In a space of three years, nearly 100 new churches opened; almost as many buildings were erected. The work was spreading farther and faster than we could train nationals for the work. My vision had been responsible for the beginning of a Bible training school by correspondence. There seemed ample evidence for contentment. But there was no contentment in my heart that night.

Through that book God dealt with me. In that instant the Lord allowed me to look at myself. Scriptures came alive and the conviction deepened. "There is none righteous, no, not one." "All we like sheep have gone astray. We have turned everyone to his own way." "The heart is deceitful above all things and desperately wicked."

These verses applied to *me*. I felt like the apostle when he cried out, "Oh, wretched man that I am" (Romans 7:24).

For weeks the impact of that book lingered. Pride stared me in the face. Many noble and good deeds (so people said), I saw to be acts of selfishness and self-glory. It was painful. During those days I shed many tears.

"Why, God, did you choose someone like me? Even

11

when I do the right thing my motives are impure. Attitudes of people cause me greater distress than concern for your approval." I mourned the pitiful condition of my heart.

Yet even in the darkest moments, I detected something good. Aware of my misery, I also became conscious of God's presence. Somehow there was assurance that God had not totally departed. In this state of despair over personal failures, a new aspect of God became apparent. Realizing my helpless condition indicated the Holy Spirit was at work. God's love extends beyond failures.

To feel wretched is not God's punishment as some might suggest. A troubled conscience shows his intervention in our lives. He can offer no help unless the need is acknowledged. This is the meaning of Jesus' statement about happiness in mourning. First God convicts a man of sinfulness. Then the man mourns over this condition. In the grieving process he discovers meaning and happiness. God loves him. An evidence of God's love is being allowed to peer deeply within and see the heart's wickedness.

What kind of person is the mourner? One who constantly weeps? No. A sentimentalist? No. A person with a deep concern for his spiritual relationship mourns. The disease of the soul is evident; now that soul yearns for healing. One translation reads, "The mourners are partakers of the divine blessing for they are the ones who shall be strengthened."

Al and I were fellow students. One summer we traveled to represent our college. At four in the morning, two hundred miles from our destination, Al was driving. "Cec," he said, "I'm hungry for God."

We talked for an hour. Al expressed concern for his spiritual condition. "I've been a Christian since I was a kid," he said. "Reading the Bible was part of our daily routine. I've always been a good guy. Never got into trouble . . . and yet. . . ."

Al was preparing to enter the ministry, but he wanted something more in his religious experience. He confessed the lack of joy in Christian service. His words flowed, confessing times of indifference and coldness. "So many times I've determined to give myself wholly to the Lord . . . and then I fall back into the old ways again." My friend spoke with deep feeling and with great inner strength. But *that was as far as it went.*

Six years later Al still groped. He still expressed concern for his spiritual relationship. "I still need God," he confided. His heart was essentially the same. There was no evidence of change. While not wishing to judge my friend, I do not believe Al genuinely mourned for his condition. Perhaps part of it was only a game: "If-I-tell - you - how - bad - I - am - you - will - reassure - me - that - I'm - a - nice - guy." Perhaps he was totally sincere; only God knows.

In any case, his concern lacked depth. Al was sorry he was not all he should be, but I never saw any concrete action toward change. That's the mark of true brokenness: the commitment to change.

When Jesus pronounces blessing upon those who mourn he means more than a maudlin, tear-jerking experience. Mourning is concern enough to take action. Such a man is aware of his sickness and calls for help. No satisfaction can be found in pondering the seriousness of his illness.

Friend Ella is always sick with heart trouble, diabetes, kidney infection, gall stones, indigestion or varicose veins. You ask and she's either got it, had it, or will get it in the near future. This woman's singular pleasure in life appears to be the enjoyment of ill health. When

13

people talk of their operations and sicknesses, Ella always wins the game of "Can you top this?" Interest in getting well? She prefers to wallow in self-pity.

A mourner knows the spiritually unhealthy state. Unlike Ella and her bodily ailments, a mourner wants to get well. This deep concern leads to definite action. If your body is sick, what happens? You take an aspirin, or call a doctor. If the pain is severe, you don't go from door to door telling everyone about it, but neither do you ignore it, hoping that somehow it will disappear.

Physical pain is one way to know the body is out of balance. Mental pain is God's way of speaking to our spiritual condition. To mourn in the sense of Jesus' word means to be aware of your sad condition—aware enough to take corrective measures.

Ask yourself the following questions: (1) Am I concerned about my lack of Christian growth? (2) Do I feel closer in my relationship to Christ today than a year ago? Ten years ago? (3) Am I maturing in my Christian experience? (4) Does living the Christian life widen and expand life for me? Or is life becoming more narrow? More of a drudge?

To answer "No, I'm not closer or happier" is scarcely enough. To mourn is to admit the lack of growth and then determine to do something about it.

Talk to God. Ask his help and guidance. The Holy Spirit makes us miserable so that he can infuse joy.

You *can* be happy in mourning!

3

Happy are the meek, for they shall inherit the earth.

MATTHEW 5:5

BY SUBMITTING

A mistake! Obviously accidental, but a mistake. The supermarket clerk punched 97¢ when she meant 79¢. Bruce saw the error. He intended to say something but his voice seemed unable to speak.

Leaving the store Bruce saw Jack. More than six weeks ago Jack had come to his house late at night. "I just need thirty dollars. Can you let me have it? You'll get your money back in a week." Bruce had lent the money.

"Hi, Bruce, how ya doin'?" greeted Jack as they passed each other. A slight nod is all Bruce could manage. He knew he should ask for the thirty dollars . . . well, he'd talk to Jack next week about it.

As Bruce helped Marge unpack the groceries he discovered he bought a wrong item. "But, honey, we don't need baking *soda*. We have nearly a full box and I almost never use it," Marge remarked. "You'll just have to take it back and get baking *powder*."

"Yeh, Marge, later." But in his heart Bruce knew the soda would never be exchanged. He'd handle it the same way as the overcharge and getting the money back from Jack.

A humble man. *Or is he?*

I have described the stereotype of the meek man. On TV, in the comics and cartoons, he is typically presented

15

as Caspar Milquetoast, a spineless, passive nonentity. He is extremely thin, 5'9" tall, wears horn-rimmed glasses and is plagued with a sallow complexion. He whispers in a monotone and is apologetic in attitude.

Jesus said, "Happy are the meek for they shall inherit the earth."

If meekness means being a Caspar Milquetoast, timid, weak-willed and a doormat for everyone's feet—most of us would probably respond, "That's not for me."

Good for you! The picture I have described is *not* what the Bible recognizes as meekness. Who are the meek, if not the wallflowers and doormats?

The Greek word for "meek" is one used for an animal which has been trained to obey his master's command. Thus, the meek are those who are submissive—but submissive to their master, God!

Being meek does not mean being pushed around or taken for granted. Nor one who keeps silent when significant issues are at stake. Hiding your real feelings is anything but true meekness. Often a meek man exhibits quite opposite characteristics. He may be bold, defiant, audacious. Moses went against the common culture of the day, opposing injustice and inequality.

Moses defied the king of Egypt countless times. After the Hebrews went into the wilderness, Moses frequently stood alone against an entire nation which wished to return to Egyptian captivity. One man against a million or more! It was this same leader who roused the people to battle against Amalek's attacks. Yet he never hesitated to mete out punishment to those disobeying divine commandments. It was also Moses who could weep in prayer and say, "But now, if thou wilt forgive their sin—and if not, blot me, I pray thee, out of thy book which thou hast written" (Exodus 32:32).

This is meekness. "Now the man Moses was very meek—

more than all the men that were on the face of the earth" (Numbers 12:3). This is God's testimony of his servant.

Jesus Christ presents another example of meekness. His own words are recorded: "Take my yoke upon you, and learn of me; for *I am meek* and lowly in heart" (Matthew 11:29).

Jesus of the Bible is far different from the Sunday School Jesus. My early recollection of Jesus brings pictures of a sweet, never-angry doormat. In the New Testament I read of Jesus who chased money changers from the temple with a whip! He publicly rebuked religious leaders. Peter was denounced as a tool of Satan. Jesus fearlessly went to death on a cross after refusing to defend himself before false accusers. This is true meekness. A meek man is one who submits himself to God. His acts say, "I am committed to do the will of my Father."

Paul wanted to go to Jerusalem to preach. The prophesying daughters of Phillip feared for his safety. Agabus, a prophet, warned of the consequences. Many brethren urged him not to forfeit his life by going. "What are you doing, weeping and breaking my heart? For I am ready not only to be imprisoned but even to die at Jerusalem for the name of the Lord Jesus" (Acts 21:13). *This is meekness.*

History records men who submitted to God, even when it meant sacrifice. Martin Luther, the father of Protestantism; John Wesley, who brought spiritual revival to a decaying England 200 years ago; Martin Luther King, who gave his life emancipating his race from second-class citizenship. Wishy-washy? Apologetic in tone? Walked-over people?

Meek men are those who stand in the face of opposition. They don't fight back in blind anger. There is no retaliating for unkind deeds. Submitting themselves to God's will characterizes these men.

Kana, an African church leader, resigned a high position. With this position went an assured monthly income. Resigning also meant turning down the prestige of being president of the denomination. Kana did not know how he would provide for his wife and four children. Many criticized and misunderstood his decision. He left because of a principle. In that denomination all missionary activity still remains under white control. Finances come largely from foreign lands, allowing nationals little autonomy. Kana resigned, looking for a better and more Scriptural way. This man still proclaims the Gospel. The crops from a small farm provide most of his livelihood. The claims of Christ are placed above loyalty to a missionary organization, personal security, or the opinions of men. Kana is a meek man, making God number one in his life.

Meekness is not self-glorying. Bob, a former neighbor of mine, witnesses for Christ at every opportunity. Sometimes he urges the subject on his listeners. When questioned about his relationship to Jesus Christ, his answers are direct and fearless. Afterwards he proudly shares with fellow Christians vivid details of his faithfulness. Bob glories in the ability to withstand those who ridicule the faith. This Christian is bold and will be glad to tell you!

The meek are those who are humble before God. They acknowledge dependence upon a power beyond themselves. "The Holy Spirit makes us bold."

Brian became assistant to the minister of a church. He was capable, energetic and personable. Unfortunately the senior minister lacked many of these qualities. The older minister was erudite and introspective. What brought the rift, I don't know. Possibly it started because the senior minister, sensing Brian's popularity, allowed jealousy to creep in. Stories circulated about Brian among the congregation. His morals were called into question (in whispers, of course). No one knew where those stories originated. No one took time to verify or find out if they were true. "Where there's smoke, there's fire," said one member.

Brian's character was defamed, his work undermined. The whole church suffered from this dissension. Not only did attendance decrease, but finances plunged.

Had you been Brian, what would you have done? Here's what Brian did. First, he prayed. "I've always told people nothing happens in life apart from God's knowledge and care. I had to practice my preaching."

Second, he talked to the senior minister. Unfortunately, the older man had no inclination to search out the truth. Brian did not retaliate nor lash out in his sermons. No attempt was made to counteract with rumors of his own. Brian told me, "I'm here as long as God wants me. Either the church will ask me to leave or God will push me out. Until then I'm going to work with all the love and energy I possess."

Months later people recognized they were wrong. Some apologized, others tried to smooth it over. All respected the man who continued loving them when they turned their backs on him. Bless you, Brian, you are among the meek!

In the phrase, "for they shall inherit the earth," the word *earth* is accurately translated *land*. I believe that is the sense in which early Jewish Christians would have understood it. The Old Testament never emphasized the afterlife. In fact, it is rarely mentioned in the Old Testament. Hopes, visions and goals centered on the land. Blessings were conceptualized in terms of fruitful vegetation, rich soil, and long life. The Old Testament anticipated a coming Savior who would rule among the people. A golden age would be ushered in, a time of unparalleled prosperity. God's kingdom and the land were tied up together in Jewish thought.

The Jews thought in terms of real estate. Jesus taught symbolically. "The meek will be received into God's kingdom and participate in the blessings of that kingdom." The kingdom of God is the place where God rules. Jesus' words mean that God's blessings are ours *now*. God's rule assures happiness, peace and victory in daily living—and the meek know that.

4

Happy are those who hunger and thirst for righteousness, for they shall be satisfied.

MATTHEW 5:6

BY SEARCHING

Joe could hardly have been more than twenty years of age. Sitting in a stuffed chair, his body seemed small, almost elfish. I knew he was having difficulty putting feelings into words. A full minute the young man stammered, started a sentence twice, hesitated and then lapsed into silence.

"I just want to *know* God, that's all!" Once he made the initial statement, words tumbled rapidly. "I'm a Christian. For six weeks every free minute has been consumed by reading the Bible and praying. While they help, they can't seem to satisfy my hunger." He stopped blurting long enough to look me squarely in the eye. "Am I some kind of religious nut?"

"Joe, you're searching for something. An insatiable hunger compels you to keep on. Would to God that more people felt that way!"

"But most people don't talk like you! When I start talking about God—in a personal way—they look at me as though to say, 'Are you crazy?' Like last week I tried to explain to my Sunday School teacher. He smiled and said, 'That's fine, Joe, but watch out, don't go over the deep end.' He was afraid I'd go too far, make people uncomfortable."

And we are uncomfortable! When a person begins expressing deep longings for a closer relationship to Jesus Christ, a disconcerting, perhaps reproachful, feeling hits us. Superficial grappling with doctrines doesn't bother people. But when the conversation gets to a level of personal experience, resistance emerges. Change the subject. Inject humor. Do something. Anything but probe into *me* and my personal experience. So often God is not everything we claim he is in our lives. If someone dares to pull down the facade, we try to shut him off. That kind of talk is threatening.

Joe's hunger strangely models the kind expressed by the poet in Psalm 42:1-2. He paints a vivid picture of intense thirst. A wild deer roams from place to place. Water is all he seeks. None is found for draught shrouds the land. The need becomes so desperate that the animal must find water or die. In the same way David describes his acute desire for God. "As the hart longs for flowing streams, so longs my soul for thee, O God. My soul thirsts for God, for the living God."

From Biblical days to the present, men have expressed profound longings to know God. In every generation there are some who make the knowledge of God primary in their lives. Where does such a desire come from? What is it that makes some people hunger for God?

Jesus said, "No man can come to me except the Father draw him" (John 6:37, my translation). The impulse to pursue originates with God. The working out of that influence is our following him. Paul said it this way: "For it is God who works in you both to will and to do of his good pleasure" (Philippians 2:13).

My own experiences affirm this. While I had some early religious training, I grew to adulthood without Christ. Other than a few spasmodic appearances, contact with any church was lost. I felt no need for God because everything could be worked out without his help or interference. Then something happened. I cannot explain it except to report that a strange desire to know something more came into my life. Stationed on a military base away from the influence of family or friends, I had turned totally to a life without God. To me, pleasure was the sole value in life.

But questions troubled me—questions I had never taken seriously before. What purpose does life have? What happens to a person after death? Is life nothing more than a cycle of birth, trouble and happiness, with death at the end? Is that all? These basic problems gnawed at me. I was having fun (so I kept telling myself) and there were always friends crowded around. Activities kept most of our gang from reflective thinking. But once in awhile I'd be alone and then the tormenting issues attacked.

It was late one night, nearly midnight. Quietly I crept into a chapel, first making certain no one saw me. I sat in a pew near the rear and in the most dimly-lit corner. "God . . . if there is a God . . . reveal yourself. I don't know anything about prayer or you but . . . I'm willing to learn." That's the way my first conversation with the Heavenly Father began.

Minutes later a young sailor furtively slipped out of that chapel. As he walked out he noticed a table of tracts, pamphlets and Bibles. He put one of the Bibles in his peacoat pocket and departed.

For the next six months I read that Bible every day. Looking over my shoulder to be sure no one saw me, I kept reading. One day I got caught. Dean, one of the heaviest drinkers of our group, found me absorbed at my desk one day.

"Hey, what are you reading? Is that a Bible?"

"Yeah—a Bible. Good literature, you know."

"Hey, Murphey, you ain't turnin' religious on us, are you?"

Was I? That question could not be answered then. But in the days that followed God led me slowly to the knowledge of himself. It was a long path, but I followed. The desire to seek God was in my heart, but at no time in the months leading to my commitment to the Gospel of Christ did I have the sense of God influencing my decisions.

God works behind the scenes. He is always "previous" or "prior" to human action. He influences, and we respond. We do not always understand the drawing or the urging, but we are conscious of hungering and thirsting after him. We cry out as the prophet of old, "My soul thirsts for God . . . for the living God."

We act by following and searching, or we disregard and reject. Sometimes the yearnings of the heart are ignored ("I don't want to appear foolish") or stifled. The desire to follow God can be rejected by fear. Who wants to be misunderstood, ridiculed, or labeled a fanatic? But to suppress our longing causes us first to grow colder. Indifference covers our lives. The next step down is cynicism. Attitudes and crude jokes mock everything that speaks of Christianity. God has touched our hearts, but for one reason or another, response is lacking. A world of nervous activities may occupy our attention. All the while our longing heart finds no satisfaction.

At various times we all find our spiritual appetites diminished. What can be done? Wait until God stirs us again? Must we sit complacently waiting for a fresh moving of the Spirit in our lives? God is the one who draws us. He causes us to yearn for Him. Yet there are also positive steps of action we can take.

First of all, admit your need. A quarter of a century ago a revival began in the Hebrides Islands, off the coast of

Scotland. While many factors were involved, the actual event that precipitated the awakening was the closing prayer in a church service by a seventeen-year-old boy. He prayed, "Lord, you promised to pour out your Spirit on dry ground. I don't know about the rest of these people, but I'm dry and thirsty." Sensing need is the first step toward developing a spiritual appetite.

My friend Buck is graphically honest. He expressed concern over his own low-interest level and prayed this way: "God, get a keg of dynamite and blow me out of my chair if you have to. Do something to set me on fire."

A second thing you can do is ask, "What hinders me from progress?" It is too easy to say, "If only my wife were more spiritual. . . ." "If only I didn't have a house full of screaming brats. . . ." Those are excuses, not reasons!

Ask God to help you see the causes for your lack of spiritual growth. Someone said, "I can have no appetite for God if my heart is filled with the delectables of the world." Many things may be dulling our appetites—families, homes, incomes.

When our son, John Mark, was still quite young, we could never get him to eat his noon meal. We tried everything, but he would fuss or attempt to leave his plate half full. His lack of appetite was quite disturbing. At other meals he ate heartily. Then we discovered the cause. Well-meaning parents of playmates filled him with candy or cookies about an hour before his lunch. No wonder John Mark had no appetite for meat and vegetables!

The Israelites had a similar problem during their forty years in the wilderness, as recorded in the Psalm: "But soon they forgot his works; they did not wait for his counsel. They had a wanton craving in the wilderness, and put God to the test in the desert. He gave them what they asked, but sent leanness to their souls" (Psalm 106: 13–15, my translation).

We can't have it both ways. If prosperity, success or prestige rules our appetite, we wind up spiritually emaciated. God never fills the satisfied. His promises are for those who search because of a compelling desire to know him.

5

*Happy are the merciful, for they
shall obtain mercy.*

MATTHEW 5:7

BY BEING SYMPATHETIC

With impassioned pleas, doleful tones and heart-rending
sobs, Charlie begs, "Just give me a chance—a little
longer. I'll raise the money somehow. Please be patient."

Impressed with the pathetic plea, the hardened businessman wavers in his determination. "All right. I'll give
you a chance to raise the $2,000. I'll not take court action
against you."

With grateful, generous words Charlie retreats. His
step is springier, his posture straighter. The young man
smiles deeply. Three blocks later Charlie spots Ray-
mond, who once borrowed twenty dollars.

"Hey, wait a minute, buddy!" Charlie yells as he
charges across the street. "Where is the twenty bucks
you've owed me for nearly a year?"

"Well, Charlie, I'd like to pay it back, but I just can't.
My wife's been sick—just gotten out of the hospital. Ron
starts college next month. Our daughter has to have
extensive dental work."

"Cut it out!" demands Charlie. "You owe me twenty
bucks. I want the money *now!*"

Voices rise sharply. Charlie stands on the street corner. His demands become more urgent. "I ought to sock
you in the jaw! You promised to repay!"

Looking up, Charlie stares at a familiar face. Hearing

Charlie's berating remarks, the businessman taps him on the shoulder. "Charlie, you have twenty-four hours to raise the money before I go to court. You are not willing to give anyone else the pity I gave you."

Jesus told a story similar to this although the sums were different. The point is that a man who receives mercy should offer mercy. When a man is forgiven he should then forgive others.

At one period in my life I needed financial assistance. A kindly Christian gentleman gave me what I needed as an outright gift. I had asked for a loan. "How can I repay your kindness?"

He smiled, "One day when you are able to help other people financially, do it. That's my repayment." My gratitude was all he wanted.

"Happy are the merciful, for they shall obtain mercy," said Jesus. Another translation of Matthew 5:7 is, "Happy are those who sympathize for they shall receive sympathy."

To sympathize with another is one of God's richest gifts in life. To see a person for what he is, seeing the ugliest, seamiest facts and still be able to understand, what greater gift could anyone want?

This is the intent of Jesus' pronouncement. He points to those who understand. Merely feeling sorry for someone is not enough, nor is nodding your head, shaking his hand, shedding a tear and saying, "God bless you. Keep looking to HIM."

A missionary friend of mine received a letter from a wealthy relative. He had hoped this uncle would have offered financial support. The uncle wrote a friendly letter, filled with news of his large business ventures. A detailed account was given of the way he had tripled his income in two years' time. There was no offering, no pledge, nor any prospects. My friend's was a faith mission—dependent upon free-will offerings with no guaranteed support. The letter concluded, "Remember Philippians 4:19, 'My God shall supply all your needs according to his riches in glory by Christ Jesus.'"

To be merciful means to get inside the other fellow's skin. You see with his eyes, think with his mind, feel with his emotions. Sympathy involves more than an emotional wave of pity. A direct effort of the will is the primary consideration. We are sympathetic by doing acts of kindness, little things which enable us to identify and respond to another.

Caroline, a person I didn't like very much, was endowed with a short fuse. Her voice was surly. Not a pleasant person to have around. Through circumstances I was forced to visit her home. There I learned some of the reasons why Caroline is that type of person. Her parents talked that way. Hardly a word of affection ever passes between any of the four children at home. Now I could look at Caroline, realizing the conditions which made her unlovely.

The word "sympathy" literally means "to experience things together with another person." Jesus Christ himself poses the best illustration. He, as a human being, experienced suffering, love, hunger, pain, fear, anger. He could sympathize and identify with humanity. "And therefore he had to be made like these brothers of his in every way, so that he might be merciful and faithful as their priest before God, to expiate the sins of the people" (Hebrews 2:17 N. E. B.).

The sympathetic persons whom Jesus blesses are those who have experienced mercy in their own lives. Edna, one of the godliest women I know, gives herself unceasingly to helping people. Once I asked, "Why, Edna?"

"Christ has done so much for me. Can I be truly

appreciative and not do all I can in return? Edna has experienced many trials and set-backs in life. A malfunctioning heart often keeps her in bed for weeks. She cares for an invalid mother, and is the financial support of two children since her husband's death. This woman can still show concern for others. She knows how they feel.

The happy people are those who constantly open themselves to human needs. Happy people offer friendship because they have been befriended.

Barry and I were in college together. I tend to be somewhat outgoing, so I preferred friendship and companionship because he seemed a loner. Barry found it difficult to respond. Once he confided, "Never in my life have I had a close friend." It was easy to understand his difficulty in receiving friendship. A man becomes a friend only after he has experienced the outreaching hand of someone else. We cannot offer what we have not possessed.

During the first weeks of our classes together I almost rejected Barry. I offered friendship, but he didn't respond. Something made me stick with it. In time we became extremely close friends. Barry's hardness was a cover-up for his feelings of inadequacy. Indifference concealed the fact that he cared too much. His muteness hid the fact that he feared saying the wrong thing.

The sympathizers are those who are recipients of mercy. Knowing God's love, they offer it to others. They try to get inside another's skin. Sympathy is an attempt to understand the motives and rationale for a person's decisions and actions. Even though people may not agree, there can be no wholesale condemnation. Each individual and each situation must be viewed through the other person's heart.

A teen-age relative of mine came to live with us for six months. He was an ex-drug addict. His hair was long; he wore casual dress even to church. At first it was difficult for members of the congregation I was then serving to respond to Larry. Some took the time to talk to him. Others extended friendship and warmth. Their sympathy helped Larry find himself in a time of many doubts and struggles. The congregation did not condemn him because his ways were different. They opened themselves to this young man.

The most striking mark of the sympathetic person is forgiveness. He knows how to forgive once, twice, twenty times, five thousand times. He keeps loving and keeps forgiving.

Arthur was one of the finest preachers I'd heard in years. Listening to him made eyes brim with tears. His language was graphic and earthy. But I also knew Arthur as a man. He often preached against sin—in fact, that was what he preached most of the time. And, to Arthur, almost everything was sin. I never recall his speaking of love, forgiveness or mercy. Once I asked him about this.

"Should I condone sin?" he responded.

"No," I retorted, "but you could forgive it."

At times we all fail. We understand our circumstances or temptations. Our own guilt is easily overlooked or mitigated. To be true sympathizers, of whom Jesus spoke, means giving others the same consideration and understanding we would want to be accorded.

Understanding people is one aspect of being happy.

6

Happy are the pure in heart, for they shall see God.

MATTHEW 5:8

BY HAVING RIGHT MOTIVES

No one easily forgets Margaret. Now past the prime of life, she had been a missionary for more than four decades. Every five years she returns to her field of labor, accompanied by twenty to forty barrels of goods, a dozen suitcases, and a purse weighing more than an elephant's trunk.

Her generosity is heralded across the land. Out of that rich storehouse of goods, she abundantly showers missionaries and nationals. Margaret gave lavishly and abundantly. Her flaw was this: she had to be thanked profusely.

When no big affair was made of her giving, her feelings were hurt. Margaret knew how to distribute widely, but it appears her motives were mixed. There was no true joy of giving for giving's sake alone—there was also a grasping for appreciation, admiration and praise.

Our Lord speaks of the *heart* being pure. There are few who literally think in terms of the muscle involved as our ancestors did. They believed emotions had their core in that vital organ of the human body. When we speak of the heart we refer to the emotions, or the soul, or the essential self. And that's not strange. In Middle-Eastern culture they conceived of the *bowels* as the center of being. The Luo people of Africa say, "I love you with all my *liver.*"

In our tradition, the heart signifies emotions and will. In short, "heart" means the person.

When Jesus speaks of the pure in heart, he gives a strong commendation. There is also a negative implication: *unhappy* are those who are only externally pure. The legalists of his day were those concerned about outward appearances.

The Pharisees implied that if a man carried out the legal requirements of the law, he was in good spiritual health. Their approval rested upon giving ten percent faithfully, saying prayers, singing hymns, and responding in the right jargon. Jesus labeled them hypocrites and phoneys. He said, "You spend all your time washing the outside of the cup, never bothering to clean inside!"

How do our legalists appear today? If our services have the right "sound," if people wear the right clothing, and speak the right language, we declare them spiritually healthy.

Jesus' primary meaning of *purity* is best defined by two words: *sincere* and *unadulterated.* He said that if the eye is single, the whole body is healthy. Another way of putting it is to say, "Single-mindedness is a form of purity." This beatitude could be expressed: "Happy are those whose motives are pure."

Here is where difficulty overtakes us. We sometimes do the right things for the wrong reasons. Our actions appear honest and good but the motivation may be evil, self-centered, even God-denying. Is there not more of Margaret the missionary in each of us than we admit?

Recently, a woman called me and said, "I have to say this to you. I believe it's for your own good. I don't want to hurt you, but. . . ." Then the verbal barrage began. The accusations were not altogether wrong. Essentially correct in her criticism, she may have magnified its significance. What was her motive? Was it *really* for my

33

good? Or did it gave her a chance to let out some stored-up hostility?

I know a gentleman who gives freely to benevolences. His single stipulation is that the projects he endorses be named after him or a member of his family. Motive?

These examples don't affect you? Ever make an honest record of your thoughts when you begin shopping for Christmas presents? Ever place an object in a particular place in your home when the donor plans to visit? Why don't you leave it tucked away in an obscure place?

I have had my share of problems in this realm, too! We'd known Jake and Helen for several years. While they were not our closest friends, the relationship was warm. Recently Shirley had noticed my changed attitude toward this couple, of which I was quite unaware. I had made several small, but critical remarks, whenever their names popped up in our conversation.

"Cec, I don't know what it is, but something's bothering you. What have you got against the Corrys? You used to think a lot of them."

"Oh, they're all right, honey. Jake's a little stiff and Helen rattles her mouth too much."

My faithful companion held on. "It's deeper than that. Lately you've acted cool toward them. What's wrong?"

I laughed it off, reminded myself to say only nice things about the Corrys from that day forward. But something was gnawing at me. Why was I critical? Why should I pick on them *now*? I'd known them a long time and never felt that way before.

From the deep recesses of my mind a little idea crept forward. At first I rejected it. I continued searching my heart, asking God for help, and that memory continued troubling me. Their son, Gene, had gotten married a few months earlier. The wedding had taken place in a city 80 miles away. We had not been invited.

Later I told Shirley why I was critical. I was hurt. "But, honey, they knew you couldn't go." She reminded me I had participated in an important activity in our city at the same time. "Yes, but they still could have asked me!" I pouted.

As I continued to meditate over the incident, certain facts became increasingly clear to me: I was not the center of their lives; I didn't like being left out; I had been miffed and had taken it out on them in another way, because it was not socially acceptable to quarrel about the oversight.

My actions had been immature, childish and un-Christian. It took a careful probing of my heart to discover why.

A pure heart is one that sincerely desires to serve God. This is a prerequisite for any spiritual achievement. It has long been pointed out by athletes, statesmen and artists that a single goal in life is what makes one a master. The jack of many trades, says the adage, is master of none. Half-hearted seeking and half-hearted desire guarantee unskilled and unpleasant results.

To find true happiness in life demands total obedience to the will of Jesus Christ.

The book of James has a section about a man who needs wisdom. "Let him ask God, who gives to all men generously and without reproaching, and it will be given him. But let him ask in faith, with no doubting, for he who doubts is like a wave of the sea that is driven and tossed by the wind. For that person must not suppose that a double-minded man, unstable in all his ways, will receive anything from the Lord" (James 1:5–8).

Who receives God's blessings? The man who passes the test of sincerity and singleness of purpose.

A young man rushing to Jesus, blurts out, "Lord, I want to follow you." Falling on his knees he cries, "I'll go wherever you go." Jesus asks, "Do you really know what you say? Do you mean it? Following me is never easy. Foxes have holes and birds have nests, but I don't even have a pillow to lay my head on at night. I don't want lip-service; I want complete service." No record shows that the young man ever followed Jesus.

In this pronouncement, Jesus doesn't speak merely of motives. After all, who can honestly and infallibly trace motives? Some are easily ferreted out, but no human is totally sure, even of himself. Jeremiah warns, "The heart is deceitful above all things and desperately corrupt: who can understand it?" (17:9).

At best our motives are mixed. We can easily consume our energies and time by a relentless self-scrutiny. Admitting we may never be totally pure in our motives has a marvelously freeing effect. It enables us to walk by faith. We can never boast of our inner purity or spiritual attainment. We can only say, "God, as best I know my own heart. . . ."

The key to freedom from the morbidity of looking always inward is to look outside ourselves. Who can find happiness scrutinizing every motive and action? Turning to God brings release.

"Lord, I want your will," when prayed sincerely does much for us. Now we can concentrate on positive living. We can enjoy the happiness the Lord provides for us. Because we have asked for his will to be done, we can rest. We can trust God to trouble our consciences and reveal impure motives.

Jesus promised (John 10:10) a full and abundant life. We can live it now by striving with God's help to be pure and single in purpose.

7

*Happy are the peacemakers, for
they shall be called sons of God.*

MATTHEW 5:9

BY MAKING PEACE

Who likes to make peace? We'd rather fight. Arguing
rids us of hostilities, our pent-up emotions find release.
We enjoy getting the upper hand and winning over people. It makes us feel superior.

That's one battle raging within many of us. There is
another. Have you experienced it? There are times when
you should speak up and state your convictions. Do you?
Possibly you shut up because you don't want to confront
people. Strife is distasteful. Perhaps you have a hidden
temper that could make you say things you would later
regret. But many times a retreat to silence builds barriers
which might be avoided by an honest expression of your
feelings.

This second course does not make peace. To run away
never solves a problem. Nor does it help to deny its
existence. We have a strange concept of peace-making in
our time: keeping our mouths shut. That settles nothing.

Charlotte and I worked in the same office for nearly a
year. Her dominating spirit and piercing words brought
dissension. Few people liked her; most of them avoided
her. For months, when I became the object of her wrath,
I walked away or simply steeled myself into silence. I
didn't want conflict, only quiet.

My feelings could not be denied forever. I tried

pushing them aside, hiding them, ignoring them. Nothing helped. Whenever her name came up in a conversation my muscles tightened. There might have been quiet, but there was no peace for me.

Then the lid popped. One morning she made a relatively harmless remark (as compared with previous tirades). I hit back. "You are probably the most miserable woman I've ever met. Do you stay up nights scheming for ways to hurt people? Or is it a natural gift? You go around blowing off all the time and everyone walks away from you. I'm sick of it!"

Tears filled her eyes. "I . . . I never knew I affected people that way. I don't mean to hurt. . . ." That was the beginning of peace between Charlotte and myself. Peace came by confrontation, not by running.

Happiness is making peace with others. We are *all* called to be peacemakers. Jesus promises happiness to those who bring peace. He intends that his people attempt reconciliation between the factions.

What makes a peacemaker? Let's look at some of the qualifications.

First, we must sincerely enjoy peace and seek for it. Sometimes we actually enjoy division (although we'd not say so).

A church in southern Wisconsin split into two factions. The pastor, Rev. Downs, resigned to go to the mission field. Most of the congregation loved him deeply. It was painful to see him leave. A third of the members did not like him. They had never accepted him. His resignation delighted this group, who still looked to Bob Barnes, founder of the church and its only former pastor. Bob had resigned three years earlier. He had been the spiritual father to most of the congregation, responsible for their conversions.

When Rev. Downs left and Bob Barnes returned, the

church split. Many of the members did not want Brother Barnes to return. From that day on, a continued rivalry raged.

After the split, both churches grew numerically. Every Sunday, however, from both pulpits remarks were made about the other congregation. Brother Barnes often commented, "If you're not willing to pay the price to walk with God—if you're willing to settle for lesser light —you just go over there."

I am convinced that the two congregations secretly enjoyed the division. Certainly no efforts were made to effect a reconciliation. Peace never comes without healing efforts.

God calls us to be restorers of peace. "Live in harmony with one another," writes Paul to the Romans (12:16). "If possible, so far as it depends upon *you*, live peaceably with all" (12:18).

Another requirement for being a peacemaker is to be yourself.

Paul was a man who was honest with himself. After his conversion he went to Jerusalem to confer with the heads of the church, especially Peter. They were the leaders. He recognized them and accorded them the honor they deserved. That's chapter one of Galatians. In the next chapter he opposed Peter. A principle was involved. Peter, charged Paul, had acted deceitfully. If the Jews were absent, he mixed freely with the Gentiles. Paul rebuked him, "You're playing a game. You're not consistent or faithful."

He may have stirred up Peter's anger (we have no written record). Yet both apostles sought to follow the will of God, and open confrontation led to peace! Paul cared enough about Peter to challenge his brother and leader!

When you come to me and say, "You're wrong," or,

"You failed me when I needed your help," that hurts but it also helps. You show you care enough to offer correction.

John and Jane, two people I love dearly, are the parents of three beautiful pre-school children. As a game I used to tease their daughters, mixing up their names. I called Anne, Susan, and Joyce I called Anne.

One day Jane said, "Every time you do that I become so enraged I want to scream! I don't like teasing. These children are young and you unnecessarily confuse them. Please don't do it again."

The words stung. But Jane did a beautiful thing: she confronted me and gave me the honest expression of her heart. Paul says it this way, "Brethren, if a man is overtaken in any trespass, you who are spiritual should restore him in the spirit of gentleness" (Galatians 6:1).

Another quality the peacemaker needs is integrity.

A few months ago I had a controversy with two other Christians. In order to prevent any further quarreling I compromised. I compromised a principle and, as I thought back on it, I knew peace had not been gained. The hostilities had ceased, the action was over. Still no real peace existed. Two weeks later the difficulties flared again. This time we faced things squarely and peace ensued.

Making peace may entail rebuking the guilty.

"They're at it again! Why can't those two stop fighting? They keep the whole church in an uproar. If they'd straighten out, everyone would be able to work together."

"Wait a minute! Hold everything! A letter from Paul just arrived. Listen to this: 'Euodia and Syntyche, I beg you to agree as sisters in the Lord. And you, too, my faithful partner, I want you to help these women; for they have worked hard with me to spread the Gospel' " (Philippians 4:2–3, my translation).

Paul took strong measures to promote peace in the congregation at Philippi. First, he rebuked the warring women. Second, others were urged to get involved and help settle the issue. Paul brought peace to many congregations. He acted in love, but often rebuked with harsh words.

To the Corinthians he wrote, "I do not write this to make you ashamed but to admonish you as my beloved children. . . . What do you wish? Shall I come to you with a rod, or with love in a spirit of gentleness?" (I Corinthians 4:14,21).

To the Galatians he wrote, "O foolish Galatians! Who has bewitched you . . . ? Let me ask you only this: Did you receive the Spirit by works of the law, or by hearing with faith? Are you so foolish? Having begun with the Spirit, are you now ending with the flesh?" (Galatians 3:1a, 2–3).

Our efforts may sometimes fail. People become angry and no real tranquility emerges. But we try. We attempt to bring honesty and understanding into a situation. Our faithfulness to Jesus Christ encourages us to attempt healing of the deep-seated wounds.

Jesus promises that happiness is the portion of the peacemakers, adding "for they shall be called the sons of God."

When we experience conversion we *are* God's possession—his children. "Son of God" refers not to the relation of the saved to the Savior. "Son of," when used in Hebraic thought, means "like" or "possessing the quality of."

In Acts 4:36, an early disciple named Joseph received a new name. A Levite with many possessions, he donated everything to the needs of the Jerusalem church. The Christians renamed him "Barnabas" meaning "a son of encouragement." By giving him this new name they signified that his generous nature was the source of consolation.

To be identified by Jesus as a son of God means we are god-like. Those who bring peace between men and men, or between God and men, are peaceful individuals themselves. These are the god-like. They evidence qualities that are part of God's nature. And they are happy.

*Happy are those who are
persecuted for righteousness' sake,
for theirs is the kingdom of
heaven. Happy are you when men
revile you and persecute you and
utter all kinds of evil against you
falsely on my account. Rejoice and
be glad, for your reward is great
in heaven, for so men persecuted
the prophets who were before you.*

MATTHEW 5:10–12

BY BEING PERSECUTED

Persecuted? In America?

Not likely. If we lived in Russia . . . or China . . . but in our United States?

Persecution looms as a constant feature in the Bible. David hid in the mountains for months at a time because of King Saul. Elijah had to flee Israel because of the wrath of Queen Jezebel. Stephen was stoned to death. Paul was beaten and cast into prison at Philippi. On and on we could go, pointing out those who have suffered persecution for God's sake.

But how does that effect us?

Leaving the purely Biblical accounts, if we peep into the crypts of church history many names and peoples spring to mind: Joan of Arc, Martin Luther, John Knox, the Anabaptists of New England. The list becomes long, but somehow, they just don't seem to fit us—neither

43

from the Biblical records nor the historical accounts.

We've stopped burning people at the stake. Flaming crosses are rarely pounded into people's lawns. Clamping legs and hands through stocks belongs to history. Who tortures today for holding the wrong view on baptism or creation? Ours is a tolerant country where anyone can believe anything. No one appears upset over doctrinal differences.

Rejoice in being persecuted? We don't even know what persecution is!

There are places in the world today where people do suffer for their faith. I know of persecution in Moslem lands. Hindus are not always tolerant of Christianity. But those "far away places with the strange-sounding names" mean little to us. People in other lands suffer for their faith and are even martyred. The news media blare the details, yet we're scarcely troubled. They are too far removed geographically from our comfortable living rooms.

How can we experience the blessedness, the *happiness* that comes from being persecuted? We've never experienced this kind of treatment. To speak historically or biblically only makes the Bible take on a dusty, archaic tone. This makes persecution a remote and outdated concept.

Perhaps the difficulty lies in the word *persecution.* It's too strong. Using *oppose, challenge* or *hinder* may help clarify the word for us.

A few years ago I was teaching in the public schools. Another teacher volunteered my services (without consulting me) to participate in a fund-raising campaign. On the surface it sounded all right. We always needed more money for supplies and equipment. As the plan unfolded, I became uneasy. She and two others had worked out an idea for a carnival (they called it). What it

44

amounted to was a series of gambling games of *no* chance—no one winning at anything.

"You had no right to volunteer me. I don't approve of what you're doing. How can we teach children fair dealing and hard work by paying for it with dishonestly-earned money?"

She remonstrated in strong language. Other teachers gave me a cold shoulder. One of them said, "Really, Cec, I can't see why you're making such an issue of it."

This experience is not one of being martyred, beaten, stoned or imprisoned. It is an example of what I feel persecution has become in our Western world. You've never suffered opposition? Remain faithful to your understanding of Christ's will and resistance will come.

Zion, Illinois, is one of the few "dry" areas left in the Middle West. For years pressure built up to sell liquor within the city limits. "After all," the proponents argued, "if a person wants a drink, all he has to do is drive five miles, any direction. Think of the revenue we miss."

Church members and leaders refused to yield. Even today there is not one package liquor store, nor one tavern in that city. Nor do the grocery stores sell beer. Why? Because people of moral conviction in that city take seriously their commitments to Christ. They have been chided for their unrealistic attitudes and lack of "spirit of progress."

Whenever we remain faithful to our convictions, resistance in some form follows.

I met fifteen-year-old Tim in a department store. "I've not seen you at church lately. Anything wrong?"

Slightly embarrassed, he hung his head. "I ain't goin' to church any more."

"I'm sorry, Tim, you used to be so faithful. You never missed a meeting."

"Well, the guys at school—y'know—they laughed at

me cuz I had to get home early on Saturday night in order to get to church the next day."

I understood his predicament. He had to choose: appear ridiculous to his friends or follow Christ.

Not long ago I overheard a teen-ager say to one of my daughters, "You mean you go to church TWICE? In the same day? Weird, man, weird!"

It is difficult to write about modern persecution. America no longer experiences the blood-and-guts, life-in-the-balance struggle of past generations. Our situation is far more subtle. Contemporary persecution comes through reproachful attitudes and covert actions. A sarcastic remark, a rude joke at our expense, are examples of what many of us endure for Christ. No one likes being labeled a religious crank. We often go out of our way not to appear too religious.

Not friend Randy. With a smile on his face he daily accepted the persecutions hurled at him. "Jesus warned we would be rejected and reviled by men," he said with a martyred air. He actually found joy in being persecuted.

To pay his way through college Randy worked part time at a department store. So did others from our class. Scarcely a month had passed before Randy joined the list of the unemployed. "What else can you expect when you take your stand for Christ?" he stated jubilantly as he sought new means of income.

It was from Dave, his co-worker, that I learned the other part of the story. Randy came from a strict denominational background. He had been taught to vehemently oppose television, motion pictures, non-religious records and secular reading materials. Working in the warehouse, he often carried merchandise into the retail stores. Randy manifested his contempt for "worldliness" by kicking the boxed TV sets and dropping the records.

46

Frequently muttered statements as "tool of the devil" came from his mouth. People just did not understand Randy. His employment was quickly terminated.

But I'm not talking about that kind of persecution—the kind we bring on ourselves. Zealous (but foolish) people like Randy get labeled crack-pots. There is persecution which comes because we serve Jesus Christ with integrity and common sense. Because of loyalty to our convictions, many obstacles confront us.

And, if faithful, we will meet opposition and resentment. We encounter these attitudes by resisting evil and immoral forces. Evil never remains content, allowing good to flourish without challenge. It was Edmund Burke who said, "All that is necessary for the forces of evil to win in the world is for enough good men to do nothing."

We *can* and usually do avoid persecution for the cause of Christ. How? We do nothing; say nothing; let nothing arouse our anger or sense of honor. We de-emphasize anything of a controversial nature.

But if Jesus Christ becomes the primary focus of our lives—as we claim he is—never fear, we'll have opposition.

Do people say of you—or have you ever said—"He's too straight-laced to have any fun." "She's too religious. She'd never understand normal people." "I just can't stand you narrow-minded people!"

"A little religion is all right," said one irate mother to me once. "But you've ruined my son. He's gotten too caught up in this stuff. Why, can you imagine, he told me —his own mother—that I need to be converted?"

Are you experiencing persecution or conflict from others because of a determination to live for the Lord? Make certain the resistance is for Christ's sake—not, as in Randy's case, a result of his own actions.

The Lord promised his presence in persecution. Peter writes, "If you are reproached for the name of Christ, you are blessed, because the spirit of glory and of God rests upon you" (I Peter 4:14).

Gary and Arlene felt divine direction to start a church in a midwestern city. A large, gray building marked the only church of that vicinity. Gary sensed opposition from many as he attempted to start services in a rented hall.

Little things happened to thwart the couple. Air was let out of tires during meetings. Windows in their apartment were broken with stones. Rude phone calls awakened them in the early morning hours.

One day an influential man from the gray stone church challenged Gary.

"Why do you want to move in here? We have a fine church. It's been on this site more than a hundred years."

"But are you reaching people?" countered Gary. The antagonist made no response.

During the first nine months the acts of sabotage continued unabated. Gary and Arlene made no complaints, accused no one. Even when the identity of saboteurs was suspected, the couple showed friendly attitudes toward them. Within the year construction began on their church. By this time they had been accepted as part of the community.

"During all those rough days," Arlene said, "we felt God was with us. When we'd get low and ready to give up, the Lord filled our hearts with peace. He seemed to encourage us even when the whole town appeared to want to fight."

Not only does our Lord promise his presence, but he commands: Rejoice! "But even if you do suffer for righteousness' sake, you will be blessed," exhorts Peter (I Peter 3:14). Jesus says, "Rejoice and be glad, for your reward is great in heaven!"

If we encounter resistance, this is cause for rejoicing. Not everyone will heed and accept the gospel. If resistance occurs, it signifies the message has been heard. It has been heard, but rejected. Such action highly compliments us. People have taken our witness of the gospel seriously. They believe the words we speak. Opposition falls because of a clash of convictions. They understand our attitude even though they may not understand the principles.

Rejoice! People persecuted Jesus, Paul, Peter and all great saints before us. But if there is no hostility? If no one is antagonistic? If there are no clashes in life? Perhaps it is time for self-examination. "Why, Lord? If you were persecuted, what exempts me?"

"Indeed, all who desire to live a godly life in Christ Jesus will be persecuted" (2 Timothy 3:12) . . . and can win a triumphal happiness in being so.

9

You are the salt of the earth; but if salt has lost its taste, how shall its saltness be restored? It is no longer good for anything except to be thrown out and trodden under foot by men.

MATTHEW 5:13

BY BEING FAITHFUL

The loneliness was terrible. For three months I had lived in a world where no one seemed to have time or concern. It hurt. For three months I had read a pocket New Testament, attended church and prayed, "God, send someone to show me the way." No one came.

Even attending church didn't seem to help. I visited the Roman Catholic, Presbyterian, Episcopal, Methodist, Baptist and non-denominational services. Few people spoke; no one offered help. Perhaps I was too shy. Was my countenance forboding? Was it really because no one cared? This last thought troubled me the most.

A few months earlier my simple and uncomplicated world had crashed. In attempting to sort out the answers, I knew the solution was God. Reading the Bible ("His Word" a teacher of long-ago Sunday School had said. "His Word. Read it and you'll never have to worry.") proved difficult. How deeply I yearned for someone to teach me. I talked to a chaplain. "You're doing fine. Keep asking the right questions. You'll find the answers one day. Don't get too concerned or too excited." Little good that did!

50

Then I met John and Henry, two lonely men also searching. Together our trio discovered the richness of Christianity. We read, talked, prayed and shared our discoveries. None of us knew much about life, even less about the Bible. But zeal was not lacking. Prayer meetings for spiritual awakening were held each morning at 6:30. We were only three sailors on a large military establishment, but we wanted to share what God had given us.

Once the gospel had become clear, I made a promise to God. "I promise to help other people find you. Even though no one came to me, let me not fail other guys who are seeking and searching."

In our decision to share and communicate the good news, we were fulfilling Christ's commandment. We attempted to be faithful as God's people in that military base.

Our numbers grew. Four of us, six, ten, twenty. Soon over forty. Being military people, many who came to the meetings were transients. Some met with us a few months and then were transferred to new places. In spite of this mobility, the numbers increased. Total revival never occurred, but a significant impact was made. Attendance picked up at the chapel services. Reports reached us of religious fervor in many departments.

We felt our lives fulfilled the function of being God's salt to a needy world. The task of "salty saints" is to be life-changing and life-invigorating. Salty Christians can effect changes in morals, in religion and society at large.

Abraham attempted to save a city from destruction. God, seeing the wickedness of the city of Sodom, planned to wipe it out. Abraham pleaded, "If only fifty good people lived there, would you spare Sodom?" God agreed, if only fifty could be found. "If forty?" asked the patriarch. "Or thirty? Even twenty? Or ten?"

If ten righteous people could be found out of that city

of thousands, then the Lord would not destroy it. God found *four* who were not desperately wicked. Of those four we discover specimens none too good: weak-willed Lot, his backward-looking wife, and two daughters who had married pagan men. That family failed to affect the community in which they lived. God destroyed Sodom because of the gross sins of the people. There was another reason, too: the lack of faithfulness by God's servants.

Why doesn't God remove us? Why does he choose to keep us here? We remain for the sake of the world. He calls us *saints* (that is, people set aside for holy use). Jesus has another name for us: "You are the *salt* of the earth." Happiness is faithfulness in being what God calls us to be.

One definition of salt is "that ingredient which, if it's not there, makes food taste terrible." People are not always aware of the force of the Christian church. The world owes more to the influence of believers than we realize.

Prison reforms, all early education, demands for humane treatment came through Christian influence.

A century ago, Mary Slessor, that great missionary to West Africa, took her stand against infanticide. Before her influence when twins were born, both were killed. She combated cannibalism. It was then the practice that after a man killed his enemies, he ate them!

Ernest Gordon wrote the true account *Through the Valley of the Kwai.* The miracle of the book amounted to this: British soldiers had been captured by the Japanese. Captivity took its toll with insufficient food, inadequate medical facilities, and indifference to their welfare. It was a dog-eat-dog world of self-preservation. But *one* soldier, named Angus, gave up his already meager rations. He willingly went without to prolong the life of a dying comrade. The sacrifice and devotion begun by that man slowly changed the rest of the prisoners. Instead of being slaves to their conquerors, they became victors. It began with one faithful and salty saint.

Salt has power only as it remains different from its surroundings. Here is where many get trapped. No one likes being different. To be labeled a crank is abhorrent. We take the opposite path, mixing thoroughly with the world and its attitudes. No apparent difference can be seen between us. But we are salty saints, people with a difference. Perhaps it cannot be fully explained why we're different. What makes us stand out from others?

Josh was one of the finest Christians I've ever known. He was fun-loving and filled with a zest for life. The only professing Christian on a college basketball team, he stood out. There was something not easily put into words. His language was cleaner than the rest, but it wasn't that entirely. Josh was different in an unexplainable way. Teammates often commented, "I wish I could be like him." His consistent living acted as an antiseptic to retard the corruption around him.

To think of men like Josh causes us to reflect on our own lives. Are you different? Am I? Do people perceive my relationship to Christ by talking to me, even if they can't explain it?

Our function as Christians is to act like salt. We are to season life so that people may enjoy it and experience that abundant life which Jesus promised. We're called to help people taste life as lovely, pure and meaningful.

When I read *A Man Called Peter,* the fact struck me that Peter Marshall was no hot-house Christian. He had a sense of humor. He was not a somber dampener of conversations. Those who knew him said Marshall radiated a quality that set him apart from others. Perhaps that's what it means to be a salty saint.

Jesus said, "You are the salt of the earth: but if salt has lost its taste, how shall its saltness be restored? It is no longer good for anything except to be thrown out and trodden under foot by men." Jesus knew about salt and spoke of it in figures his Palestinian hearers could grasp. Salt in Palestine was often mixed with dirt, becoming worthless. Salt that had become corrupt was of no practical use. Who would cook with a dirty ingredient? It was no longer fit for fertilizer. People cast impure salt into the roadway where it would be of no harm as they walked on it.

Jesus meant by this figure of speech that Christians are placed in the world to affect all of it: environment, the community and especially individuals. We are to transform the world and its attitudes. Either Christians transform or they are conformed. If we conform, our witness becomes worthless. We even hinder the progress of the gospel.

I've known several saints who weren't very salty. Fred used to witness to Adam, who ran a small drug store. He often spoke of the mercy of God and the joy of salvation. One day Adam caught Fred stealing a package of razor blades! There was some dirt mixed in that salt which made it not only useless, but harmful to the cause of Christ.

We don't know a great deal about Lot. He was the nephew of Abraham and was raised by the godly patriarch. Lot moved to Sodom, apparently one of the wickedest cities of the civilized world. What a testimony Lot might have had! This man might have changed lives, and brought flavor and appetite to people. But instead, he became just one of the citizens, living as they lived. Lot did not change the populace of Sodom: they changed him. Divine messengers actually had to grab him and drag him from the city.

There are many ways of losing our saltiness as Christians. We have obvious examples like Fred who stole from the drug store. Or Lot who became so identified with Sodom they saw little difference in his attitude or behavior. These are the kind easily recognized.

There's another kind, too: not salty, but not altogether like the world either. Like Marie, a woman I've known a long time.

Her language is pure, perhaps a little too pure. Her lips are filled with words like "living for our wonderful Lord;" "serving the Master;" "giving God the glory." With some people these phrases are appropriate and come sincerely from the heart. I suspect when Marie uses them they don't quite ring true. When she testifies of an intimate relationship to Christ, as she does continually, people feel uncomfortable. Even believers. One devout minister friend said of Marie, "She's too super-spiritual for me, constantly telling me how consecrated she is." Marie leaves a bad taste in many mouths.

Salt is good but too much salt can even have a harmful effect!

What kind of salty saint are you? This is the question you must face. It's a hard question to answer. God wants genuine people. God's salty people feel what they say. They are not afraid to stand up for Christ.

People sense the reality of our experiences. They are seldom fooled. At work, at recreation or involved in social activities, our actions and attitudes communicate. Our purity or impurity always reveals itself.

Some years ago a young man got a summer job in a logging camp in Minnesota. Eddy had been warned that the loggers were rough and the language abrasive. "Watch out! They don't tolerate guys they don't like," a friend warned.

At the end of the summer Eddy returned home. He

shared summer experiences with friends. "And no one said anything rough to me at all. Why, they didn't even know I was a Christian!"

Am I giving people an honest taste of what it means to follow Christ? Does my life thwart the claims of the Gospel by my lack of flavor? Happiness comes by faithfulness to Christ. Are you happy?

10

*You are the light of the world. A
city set on a hill cannot be hid.
Nor do men light a lamp and put
it under a bushel, but on a stand,
and it gives light to all in the
house. Let your light so shine
before men, that they may see your
good works and give glory to your
Father who is in heaven.*

MATTHEW 5:14–16

BY WITNESSING

A power failure had knocked out street lights in part of
our community. Going into an unfamiliar neighborhood
at night was quite a problem. I had the address but could
scarcely read the numbers. Most houses were poorly
marked. Numbers on the mailboxes were either ob-
scured by the red metal flag, or else too small to read.
Some painted their numbers on the houses themselves.
Ever try reading letters two inches high on a rainy night
at a distance of fifty feet?

But I shouldn't have been so concerned. A block away
I knew which house it was. They had turned on the
porchlight. Theirs was the only house on that block with
the porchlight on. They knew I was coming, and were
showing me the way.

Jesus said of his followers, "You are the light of the
world."

The world is a realm of darkness. Christians are the

only ones who can radiate light. Those outside the faith may be better educated. In the field of human relations they may be better trained. Yet, we have something they do not: LIGHT. Because of our special relationship to Jesus Christ, we bear light to a darkened world.

Jesus said, "I am the light of the world. He who follows me will not walk in darkness, but will have the light of life" (John 8:12).

To become members of a church, public confession is made of our relationship to Christ. "I am a follower of the Lord. I believe in Jesus Christ. I bear witness of God's grace." These are the kinds of confessions professing believers make.

God calls his people to a significant position in life: to allow his light to shine in the places of darkness. Our positions in life may be insignificant, but they are important. Many Christians have obscure, seemingly unnoticed occupations. Yet even in the lowly places God uses his people.

Many children still sing that delightful song: "Jesus bids us shine with a clear, pure light, like a little candle, burning in the night. In this world of darkness, we must shine. You in your small corner and I in mine."

An unnamed girl, captured in battle by the Aramaeans, became the means of blessing. Through her influence, a miracle was performed (see 2 Kings 5). This servant girl knew that Naaman, the general who had overcome Israel, had leprosy. She told her mistress, Naaman's wife, of Yahweh, God of Israel. Through her bearing light of God's power, Naaman eventually found healing. Who would have thought a captive slave could have been so used? This young woman became the light that shines in darkness. Her life was light to those around her. That is the very function of those who claim allegiance to Jesus Christ.

We bear witness of Christ because it is our nature to do so. We share experiences. No Christian can become a secret witness. Someone has said, "Either the witness will overcome the secrecy or the secrecy will overcome the witness."

Nicodemus is an interesting example of the secret witness. In John, chapter three, he meets Jesus face-to-face in a clandestine, night meeting. John tells us the Jewish leader feared his colleagues. Jesus spoke the gospel to him.

The second mention of Nicodemus is found in chapter seven of the same book. The Pharisees were out to stop Jesus. They complained vehemently to the civil officers who did nothing to the rabble rouser. Nicodemus timidly spoke a word in Jesus' behalf. "Does our law judge a man without first giving him a hearing and learning what he does?" (7:51). There is no concrete statement of faith but at least an attempt to stand for righteousness.

It doesn't work. This religious man is silenced. "Are you from Galilee, too? Search and you will see that no prophet is to rise from Galilee" (v. 52).

Then comes the end. Jesus' body hangs on a cross. Where is Nicodemus? Fleeing as Peter? Hiding as the others? Here is John's record: "After this Joseph of Arimathea, who was a disciple of Jesus, but secretly, for fear of the Jews, asked Pilate that he might take away the body of Jesus, and Pilate gave him leave. So he came and took away his body. Nicodemus also, who had at first come to him by night, came bringing a mixture of myrrh and aloes . . . they took the body of Jesus, and bound it in linen cloths" (John 19:38–40).

Not only Nicodemus but Joseph, secret believers, must now take their stand for Christ. In the great hour of trial, they openly admit their faith in Jesus as the Messiah. Both of these men learned at long last that no believer can be a silent witness. This is why Jesus uses the similitude of *light.* A true relationship to God cannot be hidden or denied. It shows.

When a man becomes a believer he is a witness of the light. This does not refer merely to speaking out about his own experience of salvation. Being a light means shining for him everywhere and in every action. The stance we take in life, the manner in which we treat people, or members of our own family—all of these are equally important. A wise man has said, "A Christian is either a reflection *of* Christ, or a reflection *on* him."

Leona had a desk next to mine. She did her work if it was particularly assigned. Otherwise her time was spent reading. The books were of a religious nature. Never did this woman look around to see what needs waited at her fingertips. To many of us in that office, Leona was a reflection *on* the cause of Christ.

As Christians we have an unique privilege. We have the light that shines in darkness and the good news that brings peace and fulfillment. The gospel claims are received or rejected often because of those of us who bear the name of Christian.

The great emancipator of India, Mahatma Gandhi, wrote in his autobiography that in his student days he was touched by reading the New Testament. He seriously considered conversion to Christianity. He felt that in the teachings of Jesus would lie the solutions to the racial problem and caste differences. One Sunday in South Africa he went to a church, planning to attend worship and then ask the minister afterwards for instructions in the faith. As he entered the building, ushers objected to giving him a seat.

"Why don't you visit the colored people's church?" they asked.

Gandhi never returned. "If the Christians also have

differences," he remarked, "I might as well remain a Hindu."

Yet Jesus, the founder of Christianity, proclaimed, "By this—by love—shall all men know that you are my disciples."

We all project our life styles. Regardless of the words that flow from our lips, actions speak louder. Daily business transactions tell a great deal. What kind of reaction is evoked when needs are presented for hungry people? What kind of attitude is shown to those who pay our salaries? Are we diligent in studies at school? These all show the quality of our light.

Bearing witness of The Great Light means warning people of wickedness. God holds us responsible to share the good news. Christians are also responsible to warn of the bad news of impending judgment upon unbelief.

Some years ago while assistant pastor of a church, I was called by an active member. She asked me to visit an elderly lady. "She's always been a good woman, but doesn't know anything about Christ. I've talked to her. She expresses a desire to talk to a minister about her soul. Will you see her?"

I had every intention to go the next day . . . but didn't. Legitimate reasons prevented my visiting. Other ministerial functions cluttered the way the second day. The third day I made a definite plan to visit. Just before leaving, the phone rang.

"She died last night," said the disappointed voice. "Why didn't you go see her? You promised."

For weeks I asked myself the same question. Guilt, remorse, pain—all these filled my heart. Here was a woman, apparently ready to peer into the light. I had neglected to go. I had been too busy.

Over and over the words of the prophet Ezekiel lashed like a whip. "If I say to the wicked, 'You shall surely die,' and you give him no warning, nor speak to warn the wicked from the wicked way, in order to save his life, that wicked man shall die in his iniquity; but his blood will I require at your hand" (Ezekiel 3:18).

This illustrates in my own life a missed opportunity. All of us by procrastination or lack of honest concern fail to meet the needs of the lost. Where is the light that shines in darkness? If God's people extinguish their lights, who can find the way?

We're often too busy or too involved. Other things seem more important.

Erma reached the mission field a few years before us. She shortly became an avid leader of the women's work for her denomination. Relating simple gospel truths into meaningful terms was one of her gifts. One day a group of missionaries living in that particular province met together. The discussion was on how to be more effective in our evangelistic outreach.

Twenty minutes before the discussion began, an Arab walked onto the mission compound. He had a small business of grinding corn into flour at a market-place three miles away.

"My wife is sick. She needs to see a doctor in Kisii. Please, will you take her?"

This would have involved a two-hour round trip. Erma was asked to provide her car. At that time we did not have one. The Arab volunteered to pay all expenses.

"I'm sorry," she replied. "It's impossible. I have something else scheduled which must come first."

Sorrowfully the man walked away. Eventually he found a Hindu Asian who transported his wife to the hospital. In the four years we remained in that area, I was never able to speak to that Arab about Christ. He had seen the all-too-human side of God's people. Our light had radiated darkness.

Christ calls us to be witnesses of his light. Not only must heed be given to this command but something else needs consideration. There is a cost involved.

In order to give illumination a candle melts down, a bulb burns out, a body deteriorates. Paul, in 2 Corinthians 11, lists physical beatings, mental turmoil and rejection as the price he had paid for faithful witness.

Jesus, the light of the world, paid the cost. His light shone from a cross in Palestine into all the world. The Scriptures read, "Jesus the pioneer and perfecter of our faith, who for the joy that was set before him, endured the cross, despising the shame . . ." (Hebrews 12:2).

It has often cost lives to be faithful bearers of the truth. In America it can hardly cost our lives as it did early disciples. It may cost us only a few hours of time. ("I'd like to do more, but I'm so busy with. . . .") The cost may entail a slight inconvenience. ("It's so far out of my way.) Bearing witness means putting Christ first in our homes. ("Unfortunately, my family demands so much of my time.")

For years, I've heard this true statement: "If Christ is not Lord of all, he is not Lord at all." Either he takes precedence over everything in our lives, including time, plans and interests, or we live for ourselves.

The only true light we bring into the world is through our obedience to Jesus Christ. Are you willing to pay that price of obedience? Are you willing to radiate light "in your small corner"? This is one of the secrets of being a happy Christian. Allowing your true light to shine and showing others the way out of darkness brings inner happiness.

11

*Think not that I have come to
abolish the law and the prophets;
I have come not to abolish them
but to fulfill them. For truly, I say
to you, till heaven and earth pass
away, not an iota, not a dot, will
pass from the law until all is
accomplished. Whoever then
relaxes one of the least of these
commandments and teaches men
so, shall be called least in the
kingdom of heaven; but he who
does them and teaches them shall
be called great in the kingdom of
heaven. For I tell you, unless your
righteousness exceeds that of the
scribes and Pharisees, you will
never enter the kingdom of
heaven.*

MATTHEW 5:17–20

BY BEING RIGHT

Ken's voice rose angrily above the others. "This upsets
me. We can't allow it! I think we ought to change Sunday
school literature if this is what they teach!"

"They don't actually say they believe that," responded
Phil in a soothing voice. "They only suggest it as a possibility."

"I'm not even willing to admit the possibility!"

I had been sitting in the class, saying nothing, hesitant to speak my feelings. The lesson that morning was on creation. "Seven days of creation need not be understood as literal periods of 24 hours' duration. They could easily be eons of time," suggested the writer.

The class found itself sharply divided. One faction, insisting the Scriptures be taken literally, deduced various arguments. As they continued the harangue I felt uncomfortable.

The argument was not really about creation.

Ken and his allies actually went beyond a specific doctrine. They could as easily have discussed any theological aspect. The real contention was this: we must believe the right doctrines.

As I listened my discomfort grew. I'm not troubled about the days of creation. God created the heavens and the earth, whether in twenty-four-hour periods or over billions of years. I'm convinced of God's handiwork, which is what the author of Genesis tries to say.

Insistence of one group to make this doctrine the basis of fellowship disturbed me. One of them actually said, "If you don't believe right, you are not right with God."

Such a position always involves danger. Thinking of this type puts righteousness on the intellectual level. It means a man's mind is judged rather than his heart. Furthermore, it means that we claim to judge for God. We feel able to judge opinions, beliefs and creeds, because they can be viewed or expressed, but God alone can see the heart. By putting emphasis upon orthodox (i.e. right) thinking, we are saying, "If you don't believe as we do, you're not part of the Kingdom of God."

Once upon a time I would have breathed, "Amen!" to those words. I've since had too many close associations with doctrinal heretics and misguided theologians to take that stand. I am learning (too slowly, it seems) that it counts first what a man IS. A person's being is more significant than his view of Scripture.

Once I thought I understood all about righteousness. My dogmatic approach was fortressed with carefully selected Scripture verses. Over the years, my resolute stand began to crumble.

Righteousness, in the Bible, means "purity of heart." It does not refer to perfection or to some special spiritual peak. A righteous man IS and DOES right. He attempts to live the way God wants. This relationship with God is reflected in his actions and way of life.

In the book of Job a righteous man is described as one who "fears God and turns from evil" (see 1:1–8; 2:3). Another way of describing the righteous soul is to say he is one who puts God foremost in life.

On the question of salvation, scarcely a Christian argues its basis. The question looms, "What must I do to be saved from sin?" The answer reverberates, "Believe in the Lord Jesus Christ."

The problem arises in our desire to follow God *after* conversion. How is it done? Where do I start? To say, "Read the Bible" solves nothing. Do I extract a list of rules from the New Testament? Memorize the Ten Commandments? Or read only the words of Jesus printed in red in some Bibles?

The religious leaders of the Jewish faith had reduced the concept of righteousness to law. "Do this and then you shall live" was their idea. The purest sect of the Jews was the Pharisees. They zealously worked out long lists of rules for proper conduct. If you accepted these regulations and practiced them, you were in right standing.

One of Jesus' parables aptly illustrates the understanding of the religious elite of his day.

Two men were praying in the house of worship. One of them, a cleric-type member of the Pharisees, offered

God a record of his personal achievements. "First, Lord, I want to thank you I'm not a rascal like some other people. Namely that peasant fellow praying next to me. Just examine my record. I strictly follow the precepts of our faith which include fasting and tithing." It was a prayer of self-commendation. The other man, an internal revenue agent, could make no boasts nor claims. "God, be merciful to me. I'm a sinner."

The editorial preface of Luke to this story reads, "He also told this parable to some who trusted in themselves that they were righteous and despised others" (Luke 18:9). The parable ends, "I tell you, this man (the tax man) went down to his house justified rather than the other; for everyone who exalts himself will be humbled, but he who humbles himself will be exalted" (v. 14).

Laws and regulations are important. Some things are more important. Love, compassion, mercy and kindness count more than conformity to a set of prescribed regulations.

When I entered seminary one professor was theologically on the far liberal side. I needled him in class and raised proper objections to his stance. I pointedly warned this teacher of his nearness to the abyss of heresy.

A few weeks later I was injured in a traffic accident and was rushed to the hospital. This professor was one of the first to find out. Coming out of the fog of unconsciousness, I saw him standing at the bedside. Tears flooded his eyes. That man stayed to comfort my wife and make certain everything possible was being done. He even prayed for me!

I learned a great lesson. A man may be muddled in his theology and still be a Christian. *This man cared.* That realization meant more in my pain than all his doctrinal positions.

That's what Jesus tried to teach his disciples. He tells them not to equal the Pharisees in slavish observance of regulations. They should go beyond. He adds, "I did not come to abolish the law but to bring it to fulfillment."

Originally, God gave simple laws. Just ten. These were never the basis of salvation. God gave the commandments for guidance. Zealous teachers followed. They were sincere men who wanted the people to follow the law blamelessly. Fearing the unlearned might violate God's commandments, they began laying down rules for every contingency. No situations would be left to wonder or confusion. All possible considerations would be provided for by doctors of the law.

For example, God called for observance of the seventh day. It was a day of rest. No one was to engage in work. Questions arose. Is it right to comb my hair on the Sabbath? Can I pick up the baby and play with him? Wash a dish? Can I eat an egg on Monday that the hen laid on Saturday? To all of these questions, the teachers replied, "No. Forbidden!"

What began to emerge was a righteousness by works. That is, if I obey the rules, do everything prescribed, then I must be a good man. They never stopped to consider that righteousness is bestowed as a gift. We never earn it.

As the rules multiplied and new situations arose, further regulations came into existence. I'm told that by the time of Jesus, every faithful Jew had 613 requirements to fulfill *each day*. All the time, the Jews knew God's singular rule for direction. All the law could be compressed into this statement: "You shall love the Lord your God with all your heart, and with all your soul and with all your might" (Deuteronomy 6:5).

Having regulations and lists of "Thou shalt" and "Thou Shalt Not" is easier. No need to ask God's counsel, no need for the Holy Spirit's guidance. No need to live by faith. Everything is made known. All we need is to conform.

Living by the list puts external control on our lives. We never have to examine our hearts, motives or actions. Everything is spelled out.

Exceeding the righteousness of the Pharisees means more than a legalistic observance of the law. Jesus knew that the Sabbath was a rest day. Yet he and his disciples plucked ears of corn for food on the sacred day. They were hungry and needed food. By allowing the action he showed that concern for people took precedence over a literal interpretation of rules.

Examining our lives for grades of good, passing or failure is useless. Being in right relationship to Jesus Christ does not depend on keeping score of good-versus-bad. The rich young ruler should have perceived the answer to his own question. "What shall I do to *inherit* eternal life?" (Luke 18:18). Whoever heard of inheriting by good works? He was rather confident of his admissibility to God's kingdom. When a list of good deeds is read he comments, "All these I have observed from my youth." Yet he missed the most important thing. The man of wealth asks, "What shall *I* do?" He plans to work for favor. Paul answered a jailer's similar question by saying, "Believe in Jesus Christ."

Nothing needs to be proved to God. Neither goodness, value nor worth. We are God's people because he loves us. Because of a relationship to a holy God, we are in right standing.

Right standing is based on love. We believe in God. This mixture of love and faith says, "God, I desire to serve you totally. I do not give myself to mere slavish obedience. I give myself to YOU." This is being right with God.

And when we're right with God, we are happy people!

12

You have heard that it was said to the men of old, 'You shall not kill;' . . . But I say to you that every one who is angry with his brother shall be liable to judgment. . . .

MATTHEW 5:21–22

You have heard that it was said, 'You shall not commit adultery.' But I say to you that every one who looks at a woman lustfully has already committed adultery with her in his heart. . . .

MATTHEW 5:27–28

It was also said, 'Whoever divorces his wife, let him give her a certificate of divorce,' But I say to you that every one who divorces his wife, except on the ground of unchastity, makes her an adulteress. . . .

MATTHEW 5:31–32

Again you have heard that it was said to the men of old, 'You shall not swear falsely . . .' But I say to you, do not swear at all. . . .

MATTHEW 5:33

You have heard that it was said, 'An eye for an eye and a tooth for a tooth.'

But I say to you, do not resist one who is evil. . . .

MATTHEW 5:38–39

You have heard that it was said, 'You shall love your neighbor and hate your enemy.' But I say to you, love your enemies. . . .

MATTHEW 5:43–44

BY AIMING HIGH

"George did it again!" complained a member of another church. My expression must have registered surprise.

"For three weeks now he's really been after us. Every sermon has been telling us how bad we are. Or how lazy. And I go away feeling guilty."

Guilty? How well I know the feeling.

Right and wrong. Can, can't. Yes, no. You know the difference. The decision is yours, but deciding is not enough. "I won't do it! I know it's wrong." But you do it anyway. Guilt and remorse capture the mind.

I've been there and know how it is. "God, forgive me. I'll not sin again." That's a lie: God knows it. I know it, too. I'll fail again, and so will you.

That is why guilt presents such a problem. God requires love, but my rudeness wounds a friend. God demands understanding, but my mind is closed. When the Christian life was new those things didn't bother me much. Now I'm older. I'm supposed to be more mature. The battles often rage within. What can I do?

Paul appears to have wrestled with this problem. He knew the right and settled for the wrong. The cry of

71

despair rings out, "Oh, wretched man that I am, who will deliver me?" (Romans 7:24).

Romans, chapter 8, begins with victory. "There is now no condemnation for those who are in Christ Jesus." That's good news!

"Think in victorious terms," I've chided myself. Sometimes it works. But other times I crawl back into my hovel of self-pity. I curse myself. Victory abounds for God's people. But where?

Various reactions overpower me. Tears wet my cheeks and in that moment of relief, things look brighter. On other occasions I feel hard inside, insensitive, or frustration gives vent to anger. Guilt pursues me, stalking at every point of my life. Is there no way out for us common Christians? Paul solved his predicament. What about us?

These verses bring the dilemma home. Jesus sets forth ideals. He's not saying, "Be good." He says, "Be perfect." As I read them, I know I can never make it. I used to think I could. That was a long time ago.

During my early stages after my conversion, nothing was impossible for me. People around me bemoaned their failures. Brightly I blurted out (I thought as a testimony), "I'm right where God wants me. So far as I know there is no sin in my life." People never responded with applause. Some resented my statement. I used to wonder why.

In the ensuing years I've changed. Now I, too, hang my head. My shame tells the story: I'm not everything God wants. That's painful to accept. After all these years of being a Christian, I still fail. What am I to do, God?

These pronouncements intensify my discomfort. Six times in these verses Jesus begins, "You have heard." By that he means, "You know the tradition passed on to you." Some of it originated with Moses. Scribes and teachers tacked on others.

"But I say to you—" (That's what makes me sweat.) Jesus actually makes his demands stricter than the rulers and teachers who preceded him. Previously he had stated that the righteousness of his followers must exceed that of the Pharisees. Jesus leaves no doubt of the practical out-workings of the greater righteousness.

Are we to take these commandments literally? No lust? No swearing? No retaliation? No anger? If so, I've had it. The rules of the Pharisees *are* easier.

No anger? Jesus himself evidenced anger. He drove moneymakers out of the temple. Labeling his attitude "righteous indignation" does not solve the tension. His tones of anger pierced the ears of the ungodly and hypocritical. Calling the Pharisees "blind guides" hardly connotes gentle phrases.

Paul recognizes anger as an element of our nature. "Be angry but do not sin," (Ephesians 4:26). All anger is not evil. Anger expressed against prejudice, injustice and even sin are healthy signs. We often must be aroused before we take action.

No divorce? Here and in verse 19:6, Jesus reiterates adultery as the single escape clause from marriage. Paul appears more generous. He states, "But if the unbelieving partner desires to separate, let it be so; in such a case the brother or sister is not bound" (I Corinthians 7:15).

Obviously, these need not be taken as absolutes. Nor be taken literally. Yet, how do we interpret Jesus' words? Can we understand without changing the intent of his sayings? Let's think about it.

The first problem involves the concept of the Law of Moses. If Jesus fulfilled the law, he brought it to completion. The law is ended and exists no more as a binding force. Could Jesus enact a more stringent observance of the law? Knowing that his death on Calvary abolished a law which could not be totally kept, this hardly seems possible. "Whoever keeps the whole law but fails in one point has become guilty of all" (James 2:10).

I do not know how to live by this stricter asceticism. Nor do I want to live that way. This hardly sounds like the "life more abundant" Jesus promised (John 10:10). Must I lend to everyone who asks me?

Tommy, a new missionary, tried living by this ethic. Whenever anyone wanted to borrow, he responded joyfully. "When will I get it back?" never crossed his lips. As a matter of fact, he seldom got anything back. Within four months he had two changes of clothes left. Debts had piled up (most of his salary had been lent out). Tommy felt quite perplexed. Life just was not working out. Instead of joy, misery plagued him. Rather than happiness, depression filled his soul.

Tommy realized he actually was doing a disservice to the people. He had come to teach them. What were the nationals learning? Dependence on the missionary. Slothfulness. "Can I help them live useful lives if I encourage their laziness? Can they learn to be responsible when I act irresponsibly?" These are the questions the young missionary finally asked himself.

These are not laws. Jesus fulfilled that. Neither are they rigid regulations of a stricter type. Jesus sets forth *ideals.* A man committed to God strives for this perfection. He has been taught since childhood not to murder. Now he is instructed not to hate. The Lord goes to the heart of the matter. A superficial judgment will not suffice. Christians are people of love who act in love. This is God's ideal.

If salvation depends on our keeping these rigorous demands, we're all doomed. "Who is sufficient for these things?" (II Corinthians 2:16). No one keeps all of them. God, knowing human nature, recognizes this. True disciples of Christ *try* to live according to this pattern.

These days people (especially church leaders) are

trying to show they are Christian but not "religious." It is the current trend to use profanity to show our contemporary touch with the world. We indulge in all worldly amusements and activities to show we know how to laugh and are not austere pietists.

Perhaps the motives for living this way are wrong. We who would live for Jesus Christ, are witnesses of God's salvation. Our low ideals encourage others to keep low ideals.

Paul knew this. He exhorted his congregation, "Be imitators of me, as I am of Christ," (I Corinthians 11:1). Imitating Christ enabled Paul to live more perfectly. He was attempting to live for Christ, being sensitive to the needs and feelings of others.

In Corinth, where people ate meat offered to idols, he found some whose consciences were offended. "Humph," replied Paul. "That's no problem for me. I can eat the meat and not be troubled. But as long as it troubles some, I'll just leave it alone so that no one is bothered by my behavior."

I used to get angry at Miss Linder, my fifth grade teacher. She made me produce as no other teacher previously had done. She ridiculed me if necessary, exhorted when appropriate, flattered if possible. But she held me to my task. "Why settle for a grade of 90 when you can make 100?" she often said. "I believe in you. Why don't you believe in yourself?"

I resented her. She demanded too much. Yet, I think I learned more that year than any year previously. She kept reminding me of what I could do (even though I did not always make a grade of 100). Once I had worked extremely hard on a project, yet made only a barely passing grade. She even put her arm around my shoulder. "I'm proud of you. You did your best; that's all I ask."

Perhaps that is what Jesus is saying in these verses. He

pleads with us to reach out, to aim high. "Do your best."

When I complained to Miss Linder about how hard she drove us, she had one answer. I suppose she quoted that a dozen times a day. "You have to aim high to hit high."

"The teachers of old said . . . but I say this to you . . . exceed them . . . outdo them in zeal . . . outstrip them in your striving for righteousness."

"But, Lord, I can't do it. I'm weak, I'm lazy. . . ." Jesus teaches the most marvelous lesson of all when he answers, "Yes, I know."

More clearly than any part of the entire Sermon on the Mount these verses point out the moral ideal. In showing the ideal, we are also convicted of our failures. But take courage! We are not saved by keeping laws. We are not saved by slavish obedience to regulations. We are saved by God's love for us.

In the midst of our failures, God shows he cares. That's when we need it the most. We aim high and miss our target. At that moment, he puts his arms around us and says, "I love you. You did your best. That's all I ask."

And doesn't that make us happy?

13

*You have heard that it was said
to the men of old, 'You shall not
kill; and whoever kills shall be
liable to judgment.' But I say to
you that every one who is angry
with his brother shall be liable to
judgment; whoever insults his
brother shall be liable to the
council, and whoever says, 'You
fool!' shall be liable to the hell of
fire. So if you are offering your
gift at the altar, and there
remember that your brother has
something against you, leave your
gift there before the altar and go;
first be reconciled to your brother,
and then come and offer your gift.
Make friends quickly with your
accuser, while you are going with
him to court, lest your accuser
hand you over to the judge, and
the judge to the guard, and you be
put in prison, truly, I say to you,
you will never get out till you
have paid the last penny.*

MATTHEW 5:21–26

BY RECONCILING

Jennifer had the kind of beauty men stared at—and
women too. She never just entered a room, she captured
it. Petite, blonde, with natural long lashes and gray eyes:

a standout in any crowd. Almost immediately she became part of our youth group. We gladly welcomed Jennifer. That is, at first.

Later rumors started flying. Who started them? No one knows, but they went through the church quickly. Jennifer had been seen in a night club. Someone saw her drunk on the street. A reportedly good source knew she was guilty of gross immorality. It never helped her reputation to be seen with Joe, one of the toughs of the community.

The first few months Jennifer was in the middle of all our activities. Her charm was as effervescent as her beauty. But the rumors continued circulating. Then activities were planned without her. Several of the gang actually started being rude.

The final blow, I suppose, was the party planned by Jennifer at her house. All of us had been invited. Only two people showed up. Some sent excuses, most of them just stayed away. Parents forbade their offspring to go anywhere with that "immoral girl."

I saw Jennifer only once after that. A group of us had been skating. As we left the rink we saw Jennifer on the back of Joe's motorcycle. Bennie called out, "Hey, Jen, we haven't seen you at church!"

For a few seconds the blonde said nothing. Then she virtually spit out, "Hypocrites!"

One of the girls mumbled a few words after that. I was embarrassed and moved on away with most of the gang. One weak voice called back, "See ya around."

From time to time we heard things about Jennifer. She had become pregnant while still unmarried. Later we heard she had lost the child. That winter Jennifer's name and picture appeared in the newspaper. She was dead. Killed in an auto crash. The article said it was unknown whether she had died by accident or suicide. The police didn't know. But I did: it was murder.

We had killed Jennifer! We never pulled a trigger. We never stabbed with a knife. But we killed her all the same. Our weapons were gossip, hardness and lack of compassion.

That is something of what Jesus means by his strong words. Not merely the overt act of murder is condemned, but the attitude that brings it about. Murder is wrong. Jesus affirms that. Since the world began, murder always has stood condemned. Jesus does not stop at pointing out this fact, but he probes deeper.

"I tell you the overt act is wrong. The inward attitude is as much to be deplored" paraphrases Jesus' words. It is not the outward actions a man commits. What he is, what he thinks, how he feels, are equally important.

None of our group ever did anything more than destroy Jennifer's name by repeating rumors. Yet we killed her. Her reputation, her name: these were the only things Jennifer had. We irreparably soiled them.

We failed Jennifer in another way, too. We felt smug and superior, looking down on her. This young girl was viewed with contempt. Some may even have hated her. It is such an attitude that Jesus speaks against. We did not call her a fool. But our contempt showed that in our hearts we saw her as denigrated. Obviously Jesus did not literally mean we should not use the word *fool.* He himself used the concept to indicate those who are self-deceived. After the resurrection the Lord said to his desciples, "O *fools* and slow of heart to believe," (Luke 24:25). Another time he rebuked his antagonists, "You blind fools!" (Matthew 23:17).

Jesus speaks not merely against flashes of temper. He speaks about long-standing anger or stored-up hatred. Not often does a man, in a moment of passion, then and there, decide to kill. The act itself may be done in a fit of temper. But what of the events leading up to it?

A few months ago the papers reported a man who had gone berserk, killing his neighbor half a block away. What they did not report were the events leading up to the slaying. The assailant felt provoked by a neighbor who constantly harrassed him. Reaching the point where he felt he could take it no longer, the man grabbed a gun and ran to the neighbor's house. As the door opened, four shots were fired. The overt act was the culmination of months of bitter feelings between two parties.

No man is totally at peace or in right relationship with everyone all the time. By our basic natures we get out of sorts. It's what we do afterwards that makes the difference. Sometimes we ignore the situation, never admitting anything is wrong.

Glen used to come to work, sour-faced, mute, and withdrawn. When asked if anything was amiss, he always replied, "No, no, everything's all right. No problems." One day he passed out at his desk with a bleeding ulcer. We can ignore a problem only so long. Then it catches up with us.

Jesus warns against this. "Do not present gifts to God if there remains unresolved conflict with a neighbor. Straighten things out first. Then come to God." Relationship with the divine can never be right if there is no reconciliation between men.

When we're not right with people, we're not right with God. It's that simple. John puts it even stronger. "He who says he is in the light and hates his brother is in the darkness still. He who loves his brother abides in the light" (I John 2:9–10).

We all have differences. How can they be resolved? How can reconciliation with others be brought about?

First, admit that perhaps your own attitude may be

wrong. Have you erred? Paul departed radically in his preaching of the gospel. The first apostles had proclaimed a gospel of salvation to Jews only. Paul proclaimed freely to non-Jews. Not only that, he refused to tack on any requirements of the Mosaic Law.

Despite great results, division ensued between Paul and other preachers. In Galatians the Apostle says he went to see the leaders in Jerusalem about this matter. "I went up by revelation; and I laid before them (but privately before those who were of repute) the gospel which I preach among the gentiles, lest somehow I should be running or had run in vain" (2:2).

Events were to show Paul was not wrong. This man of God, however, was willing to stand examination by himself and by others.

Second, another question we need to ask is this: what keeps me from making reconciliation? Is it stubbornness? Pride? Fear of rejection?

Jim and Fay argued constantly. One night Jim walked out. He came to our house. "Can I stay a couple of days? Just until I decide what to do?" Eager to help, we agreed.

We talked about the argument and about his attitude. Yes, he loved Fay. No, he did not want a divorce. Yes, he had been rough in his language and unreasonable in demands. No, he was not willing to apologize. "After all, I have my pride."

It took Jim and Fay two weeks to patch up things. Both waited for the other to apologize or take the first step. Did it matter who started the argument? Or who was more at fault? Both were wrong. "It takes two to create an argument," says the adage.

People hesitate taking the initial step of reconciliation. They don't want to appear weak. Actually, it is the other way around. A strong person is one who can admit failure and reconcile differences. He is not afraid his image will be damaged. To initiate reconciliation requires courage and honesty. Sometimes we attempt to heal the breach only to tear down the other person. We're not really interested in him or in affirming him.

Sandra and Eve had been close friends. Then Sandra criticized Eve's clothes. "You look like an old woman with your drab colors and frumpy styles." A week of silence followed. Then Eve took the first step.

As Sandra opened the door, Eve mumbled, "I . . . I came to apologize. When you started picking on my clothes I got plain mad. I'm sorry, but you *did* start it." Reconciliation?

Eve tried proving her friend wrong, even though ostensibly making reconciliation. Perhaps Eve's clothes were not suited to her. Choosing clothes might have been an area where Sandra's friendship would prove invaluable. No matter whose fault, pride and hardness keep us from admitting we may be in error.

Some hesitate because they must always be right. Jerry and I had an argument over a trivial matter. Heated words flew. We left each other in a vile mood but our friendship was strong enough to withstand the trouble. The next day Jerry and I met Bill over coffee. So convinced was I of the correctness of my position, I brought Bill into the issue. It was important to be right. Bill confirmed my argument.

I won the argument and wounded a friend. Was it worth it? Fortunately, Jerry quickly forgave and our friendship was reaffirmed.

A third question to ask yourself is this: Does the other person have a valid point of view? Your opponent at least deserves to be heard, doesn't he?

And finally, the important idea to bear in mind is this: love is the key to reconciliation. Love builds the bridge between two opposing points of view. Love that comes from Jesus Christ helps overcome hesitancy and the need to be right. Concern for our brother breaks down the barriers.

There is always happiness in reconciliation. The prodigal son welcomed by a grieving father only too aptly illustrates this.

We have the choice always before us: reconciliation or enmity. Which is it? Which will make us truly happy?

14

You have heard that it was said,
'You shall not commit adultery.'
But I say to you that every one
who looks at a woman lustfully
has already committed adultery
with her in his heart. If your
right eye causes you to sin, pluck
it out and throw it away; it is
better that you lose one of your
members than that your whole
body be thrown into hell. And if
your right hand causes you to sin,
cut it off and throw it away; it is
better that you lose one of your
members than that your whole
body go into hell. It was also
said, 'Whoever divorces his wife
let him give her a certificate of
divorce.' But I say to you that
every one who divorces his wife,
except on the ground of
unchastity, makes her an
adulteress; and whoever marries a
divorced woman commits adultery.

MATTHEW 5:27-32

BY BEING COMMITTED

The high school annual listed Marvin as "the guy most admired." He had many qualifications: handsome, high intelligence, delightful personality.

I first met Marvin when he was 26: a college drop-out, not too happily married, loaded with debts, working at a menial task.

"Everything came easy in life to me," he said. "Money, friends, grades—anything I wanted or attempted. My trouble is that I've never found anything to which I can commit myself 100%."

Commitment! That magic word! Commitment to a cause, a person, an attitude. All who have accomplished great things in life have been those of vision and dedication to that vision. When Marvin said commitment, my mind quickly thought of examples. Luther dedicated himself to the reformation of the church. Marie Curie devoted her life to scientific research. Gandhi lived with an ideal of freedom for the people of India and equality for all men.

Marvin bemoaned his marriage. "We were two sick people. She thought I was strong and wanted to lean on me. I thought she was the strong one. We married for all the wrong reasons." He added a note of hope. "There is one thing going for us. As Christians we believe God ordained our marriage. With that comes a determination to see it through. For the first time I'm not going to shrug off responsibility."

When Jesus talks to disciples (Matthew 5:27–32), he teaches commitment. If a man is committed to his wife, temptation causes no serious problems. For people determined to make a marriage survive, divorce is not an option. They have signed a contract invalidated only by death.

Moses tolerated divorce in his day. He did this to prevent worse evils such as cruelty or murder. Immorality flagrantly displayed itself. Divorce was granted, "because of hardness of your hearts" (see Matthew 19:8).

By the Christian era, divorce was permitted among Jews for the most trifling causes. Deuteronomy 24:1 had been the single authority for divorce: "When a man takes a wife and marries her, if then she finds no favor in his eyes because he has found some indecency in her, and he writes her a bill of divorce. . . ." The phrase "finds no favor in his eyes" became a loophole for divorce. In time the clause became weakened. Even before Jesus' time, many argued for *compulsory* divorce. The abuse was common after the Jewish exile. Malachi, the prophet, thunders, "Let none be faithless to the wife of his youth. For I hate divorce" (2:15–16).

The Pharisees' question shows the attitude prevalent in New Testament times. "Is it lawful to divorce one's wife for any cause?" (Matthew 19:3). Even the disciples, after hearing Jesus denounce divorce, reply, "If such is the case of a man with his wife, it is not expedient to marry" (v. 10). They meant "If a man may not divorce his wife for a slight cause, is it not better if he never marries at all?"

Jesus speaks of the original institution of marriage. Our Lord quotes Genesis 2:24, "A man shall leave his father and mother and be joined to his wife." He goes back to the story of the first marriage in Eden. God created a man to rule over his garden. "It is not good that man should live alone." Then woman was created as a helper. This union was regarded as the highest human relationship possible. Parents may be close to children. Friends may love each other deeply. But marriage has been instituted as the ultimate union between persons in life. "What God has joined together, let no man put asunder" (v. 6).

Marriage is honorable and meaningful. Christ clearly shows it is to be respected. God instituted matrimony during man's innocence. It continued after sin had entered the world. Paul uses the symbol of marriage as a figure of the relationship between Christ and the

Church. "No man ever hates his own flesh, but nourishes and cherishes it, as Christ does the Church, because we are members of his body. For this reason a man shall leave his father and mother and be joined to his wife, and the two shall become one. This is a great mystery, and I take it to mean Christ and the Church" (Ephesians 5: 29–32).

Marriage is a relationship which ought not to be terminated. It should be broken only by death; that was the ideal as conceived by God. Paul, using the analogy of marriage, writes in Romans about freedom in Christ. The law states that a woman is "bound by law to her husband as long as he lives; but if her husband dies, she is discharged from the law concerning the husband" (Romans 7:2).

Today much talk is made of trial marriages, group marriages, living together without benefit of clergy. Some call it freedom. I call it irresponsibility. The idea is that two people try it. If, at any future time, they decide to quit, they go their separate ways. No one gets hurt. So they say.

Unfortunately, both persons usually get hurt. They lose something very significant and valuable in Christian experience. No sense of responsibility has been built toward each other. If neither person gives himself to the other, each lives for himself and cannot experience the joy of union in marriage.

We are made to commit ourselves. The alternative is an unwholesome concern and preoccupation with self, with our own comfort. To care for another means we commit ourselves to that one. In the act of commital we show care. This is the basic need of every living creature: to love and be loved. "Who cares for me?" burns in the heart of us all. Love without commitment is lust. Sex outside of committed love is passion without meaning.

Promiscuity in love, sex or any area of life is an attempt to flee from responsibility.

Some years ago I attended Brian and Lora's wedding. Kiddingly I asked, "How many children do you plan to have? A dozen?"

"Oh, no," replied the groom. "We don't want any for at least two years."

"Do you want to wait a little while first?"

"Well, we want to wait until we know our marriage will work."

It lasted 17 months and ended in divorce. Perhaps I could have predicted it. With an attitude of "let's-try-it-and-if-it-doesn't-work-we'll-get-a-divorce," they made provision for separation. Going into marriage with serious hesitation undermines the foundation which must be firm and sure. Determination to stick it out makes the difference.

Years ago I read a novel (whose title is long forgotten) in which the hero wants to marry a lovely girl whom he knows slightly. In a drunken stupor he writes a letter of proposal to the parents. In a fogged-up state of mind the name of *her sister* is inserted. The letter comes back giving the parents' approval. In a sober moment the truth dawns on him. But the young man has committed his word. The marriage takes place.

Shortly after, the bride discovers she was not his true choice. As the book ends, however, the husband speaks words of love to his wife. He has made a mistake in the act of marriage. He would not make a second in divorce. Over the years of wedlock, he had learned to care deeply for this woman. His love was not the passion of youth. It was built upon companionship, friendship and mutual living. They were inseparably committed to each other.

Shirley and I have a happy marriage. It's one of the good things of which I can speak without reservation. Our marriage works because we work at it. From the first we realized that a happy marriage is founded upon Jesus Christ. He must be center of both lives. Allegiance to him comes before loyalty to each other. That was the toughest element of our commitment in marriage. It is easier to put the marriage partner before God. Christian marriage does mean God first, but it also means commitment to each other.

This commitment is based not only upon love but upon companionship. Shirley and I work at having mutual interests and doing things together. We respect each other. We acknowledge each other's shortcomings and appreciate the other's talents. We're a team. We're a unity in and through Christ. The conviction that we are joined for life is the basic assumption.

Life is too short for more than one really intimate relationship. Those who play the divorce game rarely find intimacy. Because they cannot commit themselves to another, they generally are not committed deeply to anything.

After speaking of divorce Jesus says (my translation): "If the right eye causes you to sin, get rid of it. It is better to enter life maimed than not at all" (Matthew 5:29). He means we must cast off hindrances and encumbering loads. Face up to failures! Resist bad habits! Scrutinize attitudes or behavior that retard singleness of purpose. He exhorts us to be free to pursue the goal of total commitment to God.

Jesus' metaphor calls for serious self-examination. God wants all of our life. Whenever you fail or find yourself weak, won't you talk to Jesus Christ about it? Accepting your lack of total commitment is a positive step. Asking Christ's help is the next step.

Jesus calls for self-discipline. Commitment is the road to happiness. Keeping faith with God and our spouse brings wholeness and happiness in our lives.

15

Again you have heard that it was said to the men of old, 'You shall not swear falsely, but shall perform to the Lord what you have sworn.' But I say to you, Do not swear at all, either by heaven, for it is the throne of God, or by the earth, for it is his footstool, or by Jerusalem, for it is the city of the great King. And do not swear by your head, for you cannot make one hair white or black. Let what you say be simply 'Yes' or 'No'; anything more than this comes from evil.

MATTHEW 5:33–37

BY BEING TRUTHFUL

How was a question like that supposed to be answered? It put all three of us on the spot. That morning Art had preached the opening message of a convention. As we drove to lunch he threw out the bombshell. "How'd you like my sermon?"

Jim, the diplomat and soft-soaper, responded as enthusiastically as the situation allowed. "You did a fine job. I'm sure many people were touched."

Jake, a little less intimidated, smiled, "You tried really hard, didn't you? I imagine a lot of preparation went into that message."

I sat in silence, staring out the window. What could I say? Truth would have been too blunt, even though he asked for it. Changing the subject didn't answer his question. Silence appeared the only clear alternative. At least it appeared a neutral answer.

Being truthful causes many problems which I face. Bald lies seldom trouble me. Perhaps that evidences some growth in grace. Half-lies or intimations are what cause me disturbance—like smiling when you're inwardly resisting, or avoiding confrontation only because you don't want to hurt someone's feelings, yet convinced he's wrong. These responses are dishonest and untruthful.

As a missionary, the question of truthfulness caused me much inner turmoil. We worked under a "faith mission society." It was commonly agreed that much of our support depended upon the quality of home-bound reports. Good tales produced good offerings.

"You are doing such a wonderful work on the foreign field," read a typical letter with a check attached. Those checks or dollar bills were our only means of support.

The natural temptation was to write the most glowing letters possible. Here is where deception and departure from truth crept in. It was the things *not* said which often produced the lie. Hints were given, for example, that our mission was the only one proclaiming salvation. Implications were made that natives never had doubts or struggles.

Americans have a concept that missionaries live in only the most primitive of conditions. We did little to dispel that illusion. The glamor and excitement were usually the primary content of reports. Vivid accounts were written of conversions, baptisms, buildings dedicated. Events of a spectacular nature.

After three years on the field, a realization struck

home. We had pandered to that desire for flashy reporting. From that point on, we made an attempt to tell both the glory and the squalor. The mission was then in the midst of a spiritual awakening, but there were also some less exciting facts to be reported, too. For instance, letters were quick to tell of those who made professions of faith, but now we could tell of those who turned back on Christ after making a commitment!

Untruthfulness should surprise no one. Man is basically dishonest. This is the message of practically every book of the Bible. God knows this tendency in man. Commandments were laid down forbidding men to bear false witness. Were people not prone to such a sin, no prohibition would have been necessary.

As time went on, men became aware of the falseness of their hearts. One measure to counteract this tendency was the oath. It was an adage of the Jews that "one who gives his word and changes it is as evil as an idol worshiper." No sin was more repugnant than idolatry.

To take an oath meant to invoke God as witness you spoke the truth. You claimed God's intervention to testify of your integrity. Isn't this the intent of the commandment, "Thou shalt not take the name of the Lord thy God in vain"? Certainly taking God's name in vain involves more than foul language.

This commandment condemns a man who falsely affirms a lie is truth. It forbids making a promise in the name of God which will not be fulfilled.

In Numbers 30:2 God declares: "If a man vow a vow unto the Lord, or swear an oath to bind his soul with a bond, he shall not break his word, he shall do according to all that proceeds out of his mouth."

Religious leaders of ancient Judaism combated falsehood. Much of their teaching lay in the moral realm of honesty in words and actions. They recognized, as we do, that when a man's words cannot be relied upon, life becomes chaotic. What man can be trusted if his words betray his dishonesty?

Len is a lovable fellow who will lend or give away his last dime if asked. He is an all-around good friend, except for one thing: I can never believe anything he says.

It was deceptive at first. His stories were good, believable and entertaining. As an old friend used to say, "Liars need good memories." Apparently Len's memory wasn't so good. After awhile I caught him in overlapping stories. This brought about a lack of confidence in him. Every story or sentence that was spoken brought the inevitable question: is he lying or speaking the truth? How do I tell?

Moses must have faced the same problem. This is surely one reason why the oath was brought into usage. When a man took a solemn vow it was his way of saying, "This proves I speak truthfully."

Originally, the oath was restricted to serious matters. As time went on, it began to be used trivially. Among contemporary Arabs, I have heard oaths used for the most meaningless purposes. Once, when bargaining for a curio of less than two dollars' value, the tradesman cried out, "This is my last price. On the honor of God, I can go no lower. Already I make no profit on this sale. I swear by God."

Jesus says, "Swear not at all . . . let what you say be simply 'Yes' or 'No.' Anything more than this comes from evil." What does this mean? If you want to speak the truth, do it! Let the veracity be judged by your reputation and character. Don't give oaths to back up your words. Don't call God as a witness to dishonesty!

Yet Jesus' words cannot be a complete rejection of vows. Standing before the high priest he himself is commanded to answer as though making a vow. "I *adjure* you by the living God, tell us if you are the Christ, the Son of God" (Matthew 26:63). His answer: "You have said so." Christ did not refuse to answer the demand for a solemn oath.

Paul has no hesitation to use oaths. "In what I am writing to you, before God, I do not lie!" (Galatians 1:20). This is tantamount to an oath. Or in 2 Corinthians the apostle writes, "But I call God to witness against me —it was to spare you that I refrained from coming to Corinth" (1:23).

Because of the abuse and low attitude toward taking vows, the Lord says, "Don't go around making vows. Plain answers are enough." This implies oaths should be reserved for only the most serious issues.

Why do we have oaths? Why does a court trial require witnesses to swear to tell the truth? Why are public documents notarized? Because it is well recognized that men are basically dishonest. Why do we have laws against murder? Theft? Men do these things. Paul points out (1 Timothy 1:8,9) that laws are enacted for the godless, not for the righteous. The godly will obey regardless.

When he wants to be emphatic, a friend of mine frequently begins, "To be honest. . . ." I've often wondered why. He is a man who, while not a real liar, sometimes embellishes truth. Perhaps he is unconsciously trying to communicate, "I'm not always a truthful person, but in this instance. . . ."

Are people fooled by our lack of truthfulness? A recent newspaper article reported the results of a survey. Nearly a thousand people were polled. They were asked how much they believed what was told them by various professions. Doctors and clergymen (in that order) headed the list. Politicians made the 20th place and bottom rung on the ladder.

Mishandling truth is not everyone's problem. Some

94

are truthful. Lester is. In fact, he is brutally truthful. You need only ask his opinion on anything. It is with a sense of pride that he remarks, "People always know where I stand. I don't believe in beating around the bush."

His words are devoid of hypocrisy or deceit. They are also devoid of love, thoughtfulness and kindness. As Christians it is not enough to speak the truth. Paul admonishes us to speak the truth *in love* (see Ephesians 4:15).

When we speak truth for the purpose of hurting someone's feelings, we are wrong. When we speak to injure, belittle or degrade, we are not speaking from the Holy Spirit.

A friend said once, "The Holy Spirit is a gentleman. A gentleman is never rude or unkind." God clothes truth in kindness and love.

One day while a student in seminary, I witnessed an incident. George had preached his first sermon in chapel. Following the worship hour, he returned to class. The particular professor, noted for his candor, greeted the student with these words in the presence of at least 20 other students: "Good morning, George. That sermon was awful, perfectly awful."

The sermon *was* awful. Telling George what he did badly in that manner was truthful, but destructive. The harsh words humiliated him and cut deeply. I've often wondered if the professor realized how devastating his remarks were.

As Christians, God calls us to be people of integrity. It is by faithful handling of truth that we are known. We handle truth . . . but we care for people! We care that honesty doesn't wound. The professor might have kept silent unless asked. He could have stated an opinion more tactfully, or he could have noted good points of the sermon first.

I suppose at times we're all guilty of un-Christian behavior in the way we deal with truth. Here are a few questions to consider about this matter of truthfulness. In reporting an experience, do I embellish? Make myself look better? Exaggerate the retort I make? Do I slant stories? Leave out significant details? Can people trust my word without fear I'll twist or destroy?

Did I really get the dress for $5.98 as a bargain special? Or am I one who couldn't pick out a bargain if it was gold-plated and had a neon sign hanging over it? Did I really make more sales last month than any of the others? Did my boss *actually* compliment my efficiency and dedication?

Stretching, adding or subtracting: we're all guilty. We have to work at being honest with the truth. But it's worth it. As we become truthful, things happen in our lives. People speak more freely. Friends want to share. Friendships blossom. The relationship between God and us strengthens.

And isn't that one way to make us happy Christians?

16

You have heard that it was said, 'An eye for an eye and a tooth for a tooth.' But I say to you, do not resist one who is evil. But if any one strikes you on the right cheek, turn to him the other also; and if any one would sue you and take your coat, let him have your cloak as well; and if any one forces you to go one mile, go with him two miles. Give to him who begs from you, and do not refuse him who would borrow from you.

MATTHEW 5:38–42

BY BEING GENEROUS

Our church building needed extensive repairs. The foreign missions' budget was extremely high. None of the church people was willing to cut our pledges. To repair the roof would curtail an advance on the mission field. To avoid repair would soon result in even more damage. On Sunday morning we presented the need and requested prayer.

Ozzie called the next day. "I have a check for one thousand dollars for the roof. Come and get it." He offered no explanation. I knew Ozzie's income was limited and such an amount seemed beyond his means.

Later the story came from his wife. Ozzie went to a loan company and borrowed the money. He agreed to pay it back over a period of eighteen months! A vision for God's work exceeded his pocketbook.

Too few Ozzies abound in the churches. Too many think in terms of "giving my share." Others hover around the adding machine, making certain they give exactly the biblical ten percent. Some, of course, give out of their pockets as they "feel led." Who is right? How do we give to God's work?

Jesus laid down *principles* for giving. Nowhere does Jesus demand a certain amount. Under the law of Moses, regulations were stringently put forth about giving. The going amount was ten percent. That was only the beginning. In addition, a second tithe was collected every three years for distribution to the poor.

Jesus was a son of the law, born a Jew yet he never regulated the percentage of giving. Nowhere does he commend the tithe. He lays down a principle, not a regulation.

In Matthew 5:38–42, Jesus teaches on giving. The lesson is not merely on giving money. He illustrates the principles with examples from (1) a personal affront; (2) a case at law; (3) an official demand; and (4) a plea for help.

The Old Testament law read "an eye for an eye." Does this sound harsh? It is the real basis of justice. Prior to the enactment of a moral code no such laws existed. If a man put out one of my eyes, I could retaliate. He could be killed, maimed, or have both eyes gouged out.

The intent of the law was to *demand* one-for-one or measure-for-measure. The law *limited* the extent of retribution. The Lord's principle: "Don't look for justice. Go beyond it. Law says you can put out one eye for the eye you've lost. I say, don't attempt to get revenge at all!"

David had been anointed by the prophet Samuel as the next king over Israel. Saul still lived and reigned. Because of continued disobedience, he knew his rejection by God. The king, mad with power and determined to hold his throne, persecuted David. Several times the younger man's life hung in the balance. Saul pursued him through the mountains, desert wastes and across the plains. He vowed not to rest until David's life was destroyed.

On more than one occasion, David had opportunity to slay his pursuer. He refused either to harm the king or allow his followers to do so. "Touch not the Lord's anointed," cried the younger man.

In the wilderness of Engedi, Saul was surrounded by David and his men. The captor refused to harm his enemy or take him prisoner. "I have not sinned against you, though you hunt my life to take it. May the Lord judge between me and you, may the Lord avenge me upon you, but my hand shall not be against you" (1 Samuel 24: 11–12).

The astonished ruler wept and called back, "You are more righteous than I; for you have done me good whereas I have repaid you evil" (v. 17). David did not settle for retribution.

Jesus said, "If a man hits you on the *right* cheek . . . well, you have another left! If you're called to court and a man wants your shirt, let him have your trousers as well!"

In Christ's time a Roman official could demand a Jew to carry baggage or a load for one mile. This is probably how Simon of Cyrene was pressed into carrying Jesus' cross. "If you are forced to carry another man's load for a mile, don't complain and mumble. Continue for a second." The Lord is saying, "Don't do what is expected of you, do more. Go beyond the requirement."

Doing less than required is cheating; doing exactly is justice; doing more is generosity. Doing more is a foundation stone of the Christian faith.

During the first months after my conversion, I put a

dollar bill in the offering plate when it passed. No one had taught me more than that. One Sunday morning the head of a nation-wide business was our guest speaker. He gave a testimony of how he had learned to give. In the early days of business he vowed to give God a tenth of the gross income. Within five years the enterprise had so expanded it became a million-dollar corporation.

Give a tenth to God? Impossible! As an enlisted man in the Navy, making less than $100 a month, how could I get by? I was barely making it now.

For nearly two weeks the message about giving disturbed my thoughts. Using a concordance I read every verse about giving, tithing, or anything remotely connected with money. Nowhere did I find any place where giving *less* than ten percent is commended. I kept looking for some kind of reprieve from the awful sentence of obligation.

"God, you ask ten percent. I'm not sure I can do it faithfully. If this is what you want, help me." I prayed like that because the obligation was obvious. The will remained weak.

One day this inner battle reached the climax. "Okay, God, you get ten percent. Somehow, you'll provide for me." That was my first decision. A second soon followed. Was discipleship a matter of mere conformity to the lowest possible standards? Was following Christ to be like the label on breakfast cereal: "Meets the daily minimum requirements"?

"God, if you can provide when I give ten percent, you can take care of me if I give fifteen!" So I promised fifteen. It may have been a rash vow. Yet, in the seventeen years I have known Christ as Lord of my life, I have never given less. That is not bragging, but a testimony that God has never failed to provide for our needs. I could have given exactly the requirement. But love goes beyond the demand of duty.

This is the principle upon which the Kingdom of God operates. When Jesus speaks against an eye for an eye, he teaches the beginning of mercy. Go beyond legality. The Christian never remains contented to do exactly what is expected of him. Divine love urges him to extend his efforts. The "second mile" tests our character, about the first there is no controversy.

George and Edna Severin dramatized this lesson more than any living example I know. George's salary was quite small, they were buying their own home and had eight children. The oldest son suffered from severe mental retardation which required a great deal of time and expense.

Yet any time needs were known, the Severins were the first to respond. When a member of the congregation needed food or clothing, Edna was on the job. Their noble example became an inspiration to many of us.

One day Edna explained how it came about. "We have a large family and it is a problem making ends meet. Without other people's help we'd never make it. Neighbors constantly come here and pass on clothes their children have outgrown. What we can't use we pass on to others. We don't have the best of everything, but we have enough.

"During the first years of our marriage, as the children came along, we concentrated on our needs. Money never seemed to stretch far enough. Always some unexpected expense came up. Constant prayer went to God. 'Provide for our needs!'

"Then I began to re-think that prayer. It was selfish. Our concern was our family and only our family. So George and I prayed, 'God, provide enough so that we can share with other people.' "

With a twinkle in her eye and a smile, Edna added, "We have more now than we ever did before. Perhaps the reason is that we look upon material things differently now. We see them not as possessions or goals. They are ways of making life more comfortable for ourselves, but for other people as well."

The Christian strives to do more than conscience, law or custom demand. This is true in every area of life. There is no restriction to monetary issues.

Lee, pastor of a church in Illinois, had angry words with an officer. The officer was clearly wrong in his demands. But Lee was stubborn.

Reflecting on it, Lee realized his own failure. He was convinced of the rightness of the view he expressed. "It would have been easy to say, 'Oh, well, I was right and he was unreasonable.' But I couldn't do that. I couldn't let him turn away in anger, perhaps leave the church altogether."

The next afternoon a surprised deacon opened the front door. Lee smiled at the bewildered man as he handed him a homemade cake. "This is just to say we love you." He turned and walked away.

The Proverbs say, "If your enemy is hungry, give him bread to eat; and if he is thirsty, give him water to drink" (25:21). It doesn't matter if he's hungry or not—give it to him as an expression of love!

Some years ago I heard the story of an old coal miner. While his pay was meager and his ability to give necessarily small, he gave generously to the church. The old man never complained and always manifested a contented life. "What's the secret?" a miner friend asked one day. He stopped working for a few minutes and leaned on his shovel. After a thoughtful silence he responded. "I shovel it out and God keeps shoveling it in. And the Lord's got a bigger shovel."

That's the gospel message and the secret of Christian happiness. No matter how generous we may be, God always gives more and bigger and better!

17

*You have heard that it was said,
'You shall love your neighbor and
hate your enemy.' But I say to
you, Love your enemies and pray
for those who persecute you, so
that you may be sons of your
Father who is in heaven; for he
makes his sun rise on the evil and
on the good, and sends rain on
the just and on the unjust. For if
you love those who love you, what
reward have you? Do not even the
tax collectors do the same? And if
you salute only your brethren,
what more are you doing than
others? Do not even the Gentiles
do the same? You, therefore, must
be perfect, as your heavenly
Father is perfect.*

MATTHEW 5:43–48

BY CARING

Love our *enemies?* Most of us don't even know how to love
our *friends!* Take Don. Why did Don volunteer for the
visitation program? Why were the two of us paired off?
Everything about the man irritated me. His raspy voice
grated on my nerves. Slept-in pajamas would be an apt
description of his clothes. Mostly I disliked Don because
he asked one question continually. Any new plans I

suggested, any clever approaches conceived, met the inevitable query, "Why?"

More than once I wanted to tell him to shut up (but love is never rude, my subconscious reminded me). Suffering his torments I found myself reviewing Bible verses memorized long ago. "A new commandment I give unto you that you love one another . . . by this shall all men know that you are my disciples if you love one another" (John 13:34,35, my translation).

"Lord, he's rude . . . he's . . ." and I listed complaints with my Heavenly Father. "Please change him," was my daily petition. But then the question came "Have you ever thought perhaps the fault lay in *you?*" In me? Impossible. Or was it?

After an intense heart searching I confessed. "Okay, Lord, make me loveable. Change *me.*" I learned a lesson: Don's welfare had not been my concern. Praying about the situation made me conscious that Cec Murphey needed help.

Eventually a meaningful relationship evolved. We became friends. Sharing common experiences brought us together. When his wife was stricken with polio, I suffered with him. When his oldest son underwent surgery, I sat in the waiting room with Don and Rita. I had learned to care.

Isn't that what love is? Caring . . . just caring?

These verses in Matthew's Gospel are the high point in Jesus' teaching about love. In Mark 12:30 he said the most important commandment is loving God with all our being. "The second most important commandment is this: 'You must love your neighbor as yourself.' There are no other commandments more important than these two" (v. 31, my translation).

Love your neighbor as yourself! In Luke's Gospel, Jesus points to the concept of neighbor. "Neighbor" has no geographical limitations in the Lord's vocabulary. The parable depicts a man from the country of Samaria who befriends a Jew. Samaritans were despised by Jews as being half-caste by race and half-pagan by religion. This non-Jew aids a Hebrew in need of medical treatment.

From "neighbor" Jesus progresses one final step. "Now I tell you: love your enemies and pray for those who mistreat you."

Jesus explains love by exhorting believers to be concerned for their enemies. "Pray for them." He intends not that we pray for their defeat or punishment but to plead with God for their blessing! Real concern does that.

On my desk lies a letter from an aspiring writer, a young man whose face is even less familiar than his name. I had examined material for a short story. I returned the manuscript with this comment: "You have more talent than this article evidences. The plot is weak and characterization lacks depth. But you have a descriptive power that is beautiful. Keep writing."

In response he wrote, "Thank you for reading my story. If you could show concern for something so shallow, I can now trust you to read something more significant. Thanks for caring enough to give that amount of time and interest."

Love . . . care in action. Sounds easy, doesn't it? But I've had to learn many lessons about love. We all do. During my first year of teaching I wanted to do a good job. Even more, I wanted to be an example of godly love. In the public school system talk of religion was forbidden. Somehow God's love had to shine through a life without verbal accompaniment.

Perhaps it got through to some of the students. I thought loving them meant never speaking with an authoritative air, never rebuking. "Be sweet and they'll respond" was the silent word of self-encouragement. A Christian never raises his voice. Anger never mars the Christian's image. The calm exterior gets the job done.

Within a month the classroom was a mass of noise and confusion. By the end of the second month my piercing tones matched any teacher in the building. Daily, as the children filed out at dismissal bell, I silently berated myself for failing to maintain a Christian testimony.

One day the principal called me in for a conference. "Your discipline is terrible. Don't you care about these kids?"

"Of course I care!"

"Then show it!"

I began to understand. He was right. Care means acting for the best interests of the other. Allowing students to create chaos did not provide for their best interests. If I cared, the atmosphere of the classroom would show it. That principal helped bring discipline to my classroom. From then on, those 28 pupils experienced rebuke and restraint as well as acceptance.

Peggy, one of the most disorderly in the class, eventually became a good student and a cooperative pupil. On the last day of school she paused to say good-bye. "You really like us, don't you, Mr. Murphey?" I didn't trust my voice to respond. A smile was the best I could manage.

Love . . . a word we easily trip over. We tend to relegate it to the sensual or the sentimental. Jesus never placed it there. Love was a practical concept for him. Love without action puts a meaning on the word the Lord never intended.

In the parable, the Good Samaritan never said, "I love you, Jewish man." He manifested love by bandaging up a dying man's wounds. On his own donkey the foreigner carried the sick man to a hotel. He even paid for the lodging. "If there is any more expense incurred, I'll pay the next time I pass through." That's true compassion.

God's love was nailed to a cross between two criminals. Stephen, his body wracked with pain, cried out, "Father, forgive them" as they stoned him. Peter, beaten for his testimony of Jesus Christ, never remonstrated. The apostle rejoiced for being counted worthy to suffer for the cause of Christ. These men did not merely talk sweet words; they practiced beautiful deeds.

Gene and Ella were as mixed up as any couple I've ever known. She had an affair with an influential man in the church of which Gene was the pastor. Gene got tangled up with another woman. It was an ugly affair involving several families. When events came into the open, Gene resigned from the church.

Phil Thompson, a member of another church and a friend of Gene, heard of the situation. He visited the couple regularly. Daily his telephone messages of concern brought encouragement to the unhappy couple. An invitation was extended to worship together in Phil's church. They got together for joint family ventures that summer. It was a long struggle for both Gene and Ella, but they survived. Gene no longer preaches—probably never will again—but he's adjusted to life. Both now actively participate in another local congregation.

"We were wrong," Gene confided to Phil. "But you never judged us or pointed a judgmental finger. You're the only person who came around. You kept an interest in us and showed us somebody cared. A few people came once or twice. You kept right in there—when we needed you most."

Isn't that love?

I'm still struggling to be concerned for Christian friends. Jesus won't let me stop there. He reminds (and rebukes!): "You have heard . . . love your neighbor . . . but I say, love your enemies. . . ."

That's quite an order. There are no easy formulas to follow. There are no five simple rules to guarantee success. But it can be done!

Mattie was one of the most vicious women I've ever had as a member of a congregation. Never did the lady speak well of anyone. When a compliment did slip out, she quickly twisted it to say a derogatory word. "Mary *is* pretty . . . but then if I spent that amount of money on cosmetics. . . ." Or "Mark does give more than anyone else in the church . . . of course, who else has so much money to give? If he doesn't give it, taxes take it away."

Mattie immediately disliked me. That was no honor—she had disliked all the previous pastors. Ugly rumors about me had been strewn through the congregation by Mattie. Both to my face and behind my back angry accusations were hurled at whoever would listen. Each attempt toward friendship met rebuff. She wasn't too fond of the officers either. Frankly, I avoided that woman as much as possible. Until October.

A routine medical check-up in October. The result: cancer. No one told Mattie it was terminal. People came to offer comfort or volunteer to clean house, even to bring food. They left either in anger or hurt. She would tolerate no sympathy or assistance from anyone.

But slowly during the seven months Mattie lingered, I learned to care for her. First, I prayed daily for both of us. "God, give me love for that sister. Help my care to be genuine. Create a response in her heart."

Second, I tried to see circumstances through her eyes. Here lay a dying woman (she knew it even though no one ever said it). During twenty-three years of childless marriage, Jim had shown almost no affection for his wife.

Financial problems because of poor management strained their relationship. A number of other factors came to light over the months. The picture of a needy person emerged.

Besides daily prayer, I visited her regularly. Every physical comfort our church could offer was made available and insisted upon. Women of the congregation came weekly to clean. Mondays and Thursdays hot meals were carried in.

How does love act? That was the question to be wrestled with. No warm or tender feeling stirred me. There was only a sense of realizing a need. I attempted to act as love would act.

Somewhere during the months I learned to care. We became friends. Mattie maintained a vile disposition until the end. No radical transformation came over her character. But in ministering out of concern, I learned to understand. When she died, my tears were genuine.

Love often must be learned. It does not always come easy. The hardest example of that happened to us on the mission field. A teacher in one of our schools there had sexually assaulted two of our high school girls. When faced with the evidence, the teacher denied it. When confronted he stood with a group of school boys, anger distorting their features. He refused to send them away so he and I could talk privately. Before I could make an accusation, he struck me, knocking me to the ground. One of the boys broke my glasses. Another grabbed a lamp and emptied the kerosene all over me. They intended to set me on fire. The only thing that saved my life was that no one had matches.

Perhaps in searching for matches Efram had time to think over what he was doing. "Stop! We've done enough!" he cried. Then the teacher ran from the scene. By morning no trace of the man could be found. Rumors circulated that he had gone to the Serengeti plains. No one knew for sure.

"God, change Efram's heart," was our continual prayer. It took time to heal the wounds from the beating. It took longer for my anger to heal and genuine concern to take root. "Lord, help Efram" was then prayed with honest compassion.

Three years later our work had spread into the region of the Serengeti. Several new churches opened. My wife conducted the first women's convention of that district. At the close of the services she looked up to see Efram walk into the mud-and-thatch building. He came toward her. Shirley gasped with fear.

"Don't be afraid, Mrs. Murphey," he said softly. "I won't hurt you."

"Wha-what do you want?"

"To ask forgiveness. I am now a Christian. I've been afraid to ask you to forgive. Will you?"

"Yes, I will . . . so will my husband . . . *brother,*" she said, clasping his hand.

Jesus said, "Love your enemies. Pray for them." In loving and praying, both parties benefit. You gain insight about yourself. God helps you understand the other. And mutual understanding is the real key to love.

And love, which can transform all things, can make you happy.

18

A CHOCOLATE PARABLE

Two miracles occurred that Wednesday afternoon. First, Billy had a nickel. Second, we walked out of Neugebaur's store with a Hershey bar.

You have to understand that those two events happened in a poor section of a midwestern city during World War II. Ten-year olds in our neighborhood just didn't have nickels to spend!

And chocolate? Hershey bars and Peter Paul Mounds were as scarce as genuine moon stones are today. When Mr. Neugebaur did get a supply, he hid them under the counter and secreted them for only his best customers.

And if I'm counting miracles, it was certainly more than a stroke of good luck that Billy and I had patched up our week-long quarrel that morning and that I walked out of the store with him. Billy even promised me half of the chocolate squares (minus two because he paid for the candy).

We paused under the scrubby oak in the vacant lot next to the store. We had planned to sit down and spend at least an hour sucking on the delicious milk chocolate. (None of us ever *chewed*. That made the chocolate disappear too quickly.)

111

That's when Gilbert and Roland came up. We didn't like either of them—and neither did any of the other kids in our neighborhood. Both almost six feet tall. Both in the fourth grade with Billy and me. Both physically strong and bullies. Gilbert was probably dumber than Roland, but neither read beyond the second-grade level.

"Billy, gimme that Hershey!" Gilbert commanded. "I ain't had none for a long time!"

"It's mine. Mama gave me this nickel for helping out at the house this morning."

"Yeah, Gilbert, leave 'em alone!" Roland yelled. "*I'll* eat the Hershey!"

"Yeah? You and whose army? I seen it first. I seen him comin' outta the store. *I* get the Hershey!"

"Over my dead body!" And Gilbert moved toward us.

Then Roland pushed Gilbert. He stumbled against the oak tree and rolled over. Instantly he jumped to his feet and sprinted toward Roland. He whacked Roland across the back of the head. Roland turned around and punched Gilbert in the jaw. Gilbert returned the blow.

They stopped long enough to yell at each other. Then they moved away, and began circling. Both put their hands in the boxer's position, waiting for the other to attack. Gilbert lunged, Roland caught him by the neck and held on. They fell to the ground and rolled in the dust.

Billy pulled me by the arm and we sat down on the grass near the oak tree. With hands behind him, Billy slipped the chocolate out of the outer wrapper and then from the inner-white wrapper. He then inserted the inner wrapper back inside the brown wrapper. He laid it on the ground two feet in front of him.

I watched his actions from the corner of my eye. With hands still behind his back, Billy broke off three squares of chocolate. He handed them to me. Then broke off

112

four for himself. I held two in my hand while I sucked the third piece of sweet chocolate.

Of course, after we made sure that both Gilbert and Roland saw the now-empty wrapper on the ground, Billy and I hurried on to his house. We spent the afternoon on his back porch sucking chocolate squares.

In some ways, the Sermon on the Mount reminds me of that incident.

For years I read the commentators of Matthew's gospel. They held up warning signals: no trespassing on chapters five through seven! Do not enter! Not for the Christian Church!

Some referred to these passages as the Magna Carta of the Kingdom—referring to a time when they believed Jesus would live and rule on earth for a thousand years. This section, they declared, is God's code of ethics for that period.

A famous nineteenth-century theologian called it "an interim ethic" meaning ethical guidelines for the church until the second coming of Jesus Christ.

"Oh, no!" exclaimed another. "These teachings are eternal. But you have to look at the literary composition. You see, some obscure writer compiled five different discourses, covering what we now have as Matthew five through seven. He arranged them systematically. . . ."

Another scholar emerges. "Wait! You've missed it, too!"

He explains in pedantic terms that the Sermon on the Mount is "The Proclamation through the mouth of Jesus of the Conditions of Entrance into the Kingdom Ordained by God."

As in most matters concerning the doctrinal meaning of Scripture, there are arguments: "It's the manifesto of the King!" "No! Let's call it the Compendium of Christ's

Doctrine." "Both wrong! You don't get the idea at all!" cries out another voice.

One has marginal notes printed in his favorite Bible to prove his point. "See! See!"

"No, we don't!" several voices ring out.

"Then you don't understand the Bible at all. Jesus preached the kingdom message. If the Jews had repented and turned to Jesus, then the Sermon on the Mount would have become the ethical standards for the inaugurated kingdom. But, unfortunately, the Jews rejected Jesus. He died on a cross and so these instructions have been withdrawn until Jesus Christ returns."

Another voice silences him.

Perhaps the scholars are like the blind men from Hindustan who encountered their first elephant. Each stood at a different location around the elephant. Each man described what he felt. Each was right—but wrong, too.

Each man decided his little ray of understanding described the whole.

So I'm no longer listening to the squabbling scholars.

I'm remembering when Billy and I sat and sucked chocolate squares on a summer day.

I'm content to let the learned argue. We need the scholarship. The research. We need the help they provide in better understanding the literary and historical settings. But so often they still remind me of Roland and Gilbert fighting for Billy's chocolate.

When I read portions of the Bible that make me happy in my Christian faith, and strengthen me in my day-to-day existence, I'm satisfied.

As far as I'm concerned, God speaks to me in the Bible through the Holy Spirit.

He may use portions of the Bible originally meant for Abraham or Zephaniah or Bildad the Shuhite. But they're still good words. And when God makes those words alive for Cec Murphey—then I don't worry about the question of interim ethics or a far-off period.

I've found help for now.

For me, the Sermon on the Mount provides comfort. It encourages me.

When Jesus says, "Happy *are* those who hunger and thirst after righteousness," I'm willing to accept that pronouncement at face value. Not a promise for the future. Not a system of doctrine for a special group or a millenial period.

It's the word for Cec Murphey for his needs in his own time.

That gives me peace.

That enables me to be strong and secure.

It will help you, too, to **put on a happy faith!**